What people are saying about *Kol Halev*

"*Kol Halev: A Jewish Chaplain's Handbook* is a wonderful compilation of essential prayers and rituals used by clergy during some of life's most delicate moments. The easy-to-use volume covers moments of birth, death, and uncertainty with sensitivity, attentiveness, and wisdom. This book will certainly be a vital resource for chaplains and rabbis. And I am extremely proud to say that the authors, Rabbi M Chava Evans and Rabbi Eryn London, are graduates of Yeshivat Maharat!"

Rabba Sara Hurwitz, President and Co-Founder, Yeshivat Maharat

"Hospital Chaplaincies often ask me if there's a book specifically designed for Jewish chaplains and caregivers supporting their patients. Until *Kol Ha Lev*, I knew of none. Chava and Eryn have created an invaluable resource. This comprehensive guide combines traditional and original Jewish prayers, offering tools to address diverse spiritual needs. It also bravely provides a menu of suggestions for modern Jewish Chaplains in public spaces to best serve patients of all faiths and none, leaving the choice to the user. I highly recommend *Kol Ha Lev*."

Rabbi Alex Goldberg, Dean of Religious Life and Belief, Surrey University

"It is inspirational to be aware of the years of experience which have gone into compiling this essential resource for all practitioners of Jewish pastoral and hospital work. At its heart are deeply moving and spiritual original prayers composed by the authors themselves. 'I try to remind my colleagues and patients that they themselves are sources of blessing.' (Rabbi M. Chava Evans)"

Rabbi Michael Hilton, author, Rabbi Emeritus of Kol Chai Hatch End Reform Jewish Community, a lecturer at Leo Baeck College London and a Honorary Research Fellow of the Centre for Jewish Studies, University of Manchester.

"Rabbi Eryn and Rabbi Chava have lovingly crafted a much needed resource for Jewish chaplains and CPE students. With both traditional and creative resources, this book walks with the chaplain in navigating how we offer compassionate professional chaplaincy to patients, families, and staff of all faiths. Informed by extensive experience and heart, this is a wonderful contribution to Jewish spiritual care and to the wider field of chaplaincy!"

Rabbanit Alissa Thomas-Newborn, BCC
President-Elect of Neshama Association of Jewish Chaplains, Hospital Chaplain, and Congregational Rabbanit

"The book will be a true balm for patients and their families"

Reverend Daniel H. Yang, Chaplain at New York-Presbyterian Hospital

"Clear! Concise! Informative! Inspirational! Rabbi Evans and Rabbi London have given the 'Spiritual Care World' a valuable tool! Whether you are of the Jewish faith or not, you will be blessed and better equipped to serve others with *Kol Ha Lev: A Jewish Chaplain's Handbook*!"

Reverend Jules Christian, Pastor, Chaplain, Writer, and Counselor

"A wonderful resource for Jewish health care chaplains and for those working in multifaith care. Fully comprehensive, covering many prayers and situations and scenarios that may arise with compassion in a user-friendly format all in one place! This is a very needed part of any chaplains' collection. I shall be recommending it to all my colleagues."

Dr. Harrie Cedar, Healthcare Chaplain at Guys and St Thomas' Hospital, as well as the Jewish Chaplain at King's College of London

Kol Ha Lev: A Jewish Chaplain's Handbook

By: Rabbi M. Chava Evans
& Rabbi Eryn London

Lioness

Publisher: Lioness Books

Editor: Rachel Cohen Yeshurun
Cover Designer: Noa Evron
Internal Design: Noa Evron, Gilad Visotsky

IN LIBRARY IN-DATA-PUBLICATION

 Kol Ha Lev: A Jewish Chaplain's Handbook
Rabbi M. Chava Evans & Rabbi Eryn London
p. cm.
ISBN: 978-1-957712-10-9 (print) ISBN: 978-1-957712-09-3 (ebook)

1. Religion   2. Spirituality   3. Judaism

Dedication

In honor of Sheila E. Klein
for supporting this project through
Maharat's Entrepreneurial Micro Grant

In loving and everlasting memory of
Stanley I. Rosenzweig by his wife, Zelda R. Stern.

Contents

Acknowledgments

From Rabbi Eryn

I would like to thank Chava for having a really great idea for a necessary tool and bringing me on board. Michael and Ellie for a whole load of things that are too long to list. My CPE supervisors, residency cohorts, and chaplain colleagues for teaching me and helping me learn and grow and as a chaplain and person. Yeshiva Maharat and Sheila for ensuring that this project can happen. And to Elana and her amazing team for making an idea into a real book.

From Rabbi M. Chava

Thank you to my partner Kim for all her support, whether by giving me writing advice or cheering me on. Thank you to my children for being untiringly inspirational. Thank you to Rabbi Eryn London for the wonderful experience of making this book. Thanks to Mirim Udel and Carmella Abraham for their friendship through trying times. Many, many thanks to Sheila Klein for making this book possible and to Rabbanit Sara Hurwitz for her unending support. And finally thank you to my parents who raised me in a family that loved books and writing.

Introductions from the Authors

From Rabbi M. Chava Evans

I love to bless people. It's a simple gift that I can give. In fact, I bless people so frequently and with such fervor – only after asking permission to give the blessing, of course – that the staff at the hospital where I work have a special name for my blessings: they call them "drive-by blessings." This moniker was adopted among my friends in the food services, transportation, and house-keeping divisions because they know that if they pass me coming down one of the long white corridors, I will ask, "Friend, would you like a blessing today?" When people stop me in the halls for a blessing, I often respond with the three verses of the Priestly blessing, (Num. 6:24-26), first in English and then in the original Hebrew. Reciting the Hebrew feels authentic to me, and I have been told that hearing the prayer in the original language adds solemnity to the beautiful little shared moment.

Those I bless are those who bless me. I will frequently ask the recipient of my blessings to bless me back in their own words. In doing so, I hope to remind my colleagues and patients that they themselves are sources of blessing and that they, too, have the ability to bless all those with whom they come in contact.

The power of this work came to the fore during my work with one particular family. Since my ordination in 2017 from Yeshivat Maharat, I had been working for a local Jewish agency and found myself accompanying a family during a painful journey in which the husband/father went through a long illness and ultimately a difficult death. I spent a year attending to the family during their traumas and torment. I learned many lessons about life, connection, and myself, and decided that I very much wanted to continue this sacred work. You might say that I found my calling.

I quit my job and began my journey as a chaplain. I began at Adventist HealthCare Shady Grove Medical Center in Rockville,

Maryland. During my years-long process training as a chaplain, I did work-study at the NIH, at Medstar Georgetown University Hospital, at a local Jewish hospice as a hospice rabbi and chaplain, at Holy Cross hospital in Silver Spring, and at Ascension St. Agnes in Baltimore where I continued to work.

In each of these places, some of which are Catholic institutions, I was the only Jewish chaplain on the premises. I found myself serving both Jewish and non-Jewish patients in emergency situations, often in acute care environments. There is a wealth of handbooks for non-Jewish chaplains, and I quickly became adept at using them and adapting the liturgies so I could say them as a Jew. But that did not always work. I had experiences of being called to officiate at 4AM death beds, desperately searching for materials in the middle of the night and not finding them. I knew that I never wanted to have that kind of experience unprepared.

I began collecting my own resources of Jewish liturgical material that was appropriate to use in acute care settings. Also, since American Orthodox Jews do not have a rich tradition of extemporaneous prayer in English, I had to learn that skill. I would often write down my prayers before I entered a room, and I collected those as well.

This book is a collection of those – Jewish liturgies gathered and repurposed, my own original prayers, and adapted Christian prayers.

The adaptations of Christian prayers were done in consultation with my Catholic and Protestant colleagues with whom I worked most closely. I did not use the other traditions because I did not yet have a close working relationship with chaplains of those faiths and did not feel comfortable doing this without their input. I hope to create those collaborations in a later iteration of this project. Clearly this is a work in progress, and I continue to grow along with my collection of texts and insights.

From Rabbi Eryn London

In some ways I was working in pastoral care before I even knew the term, and long before I started my studies to be a rabbi and a chaplain. I remember one summer when I was working in a camp and I was talking about my past work and interests with another rabbi who works in chaplaincy, and she said, "That sounds exactly like pastoral care and chaplaincy. You should do Clinical Pastoral Education (CPE)". That comment was a turning point for me in thinking about what I wanted my rabbinate to look like.

I have had a rich variety of professional experiences that led me to this point. I have worked in a children's hospital with patients and their families, done medical clowning in a geriatric unit in a hospital, organized volunteer programs in senior living facilities, and run an intergenerational theater program. I also worked as a therapeutic recreation specialist in a senior living facility, while offering a listening ear to residents and their families and facilitating monthly intergenerational Kabbalat Shabbat services. I was constantly finding myself in situations where people would share their stories and concerns. Often, people would approach me with a halachic question that quickly evolved into a deeper conversation.

The summer before my last year of rabbinical school, I did a unit of CPE at Columbia Presbyterian Hospital. Much of the job felt familiar to me, as the rabbi told me – but probably the most unfamiliar part was crafting and reciting spontaneous prayers with people. This skill was not taught to me in any of my years of Jewish education or rabbinical studies. Prayer seemed to be something made up of fixed words and times. It was new for me to experience a conversation with another person as an opportunity to call out to Gd in prayer – and to be the one to formulate that prayer.

Following my ordination from Yeshivat Maharat in 2017, I did two years of residency at NewYork-Presbyterian/Weil Cornell Medical

Center. I worked with people of all faiths and of no faith, offering emotional and spiritual support to patients, families, and staff. In that role of working full-time as a chaplain, I was called often to pray with people, which meant creating prayer at a moment's notice or knowing texts to fit all occasions.

Often, I found that when it came to Jewish prayers, I needed to carry at least three different resource books – none of which had everything I needed. They were helpful, though, each serving as a building block when I was working with people. It was useful to have a structure that, at least for me, felt familiar. Based on this structure, I could move some words around, leave some parts out, add words that I knew would be meaningful, or just get an idea of what someone else had written and thought about. All of this was helpful, especially in the moments of crisis.

When Rabbi Chava asked me to collaborate with her on a book of prayers for chaplains, I immediately agreed. There was a great need for a book that held all those parts of prayers in one place: that had Hebrew transliteration and translation; that showed a mix of traditional prayers as well as self-written prayers; and that told the stories to inspire others to create prayerful spaces – even when coming from an Orthodox Jewish background.

I hope this book serves that purpose well, and that my colleagues around the world find this volume useful as they do their sacred work as chaplains.

How to use this book

This book is intended for Jewish chaplains in health care settings who have Jewish, Christian, and other patients and who need resources in their prayer work.

The book includes traditional prayers, adapted prayers, and original prayers. Along with the prayers, you will find background information, anecdotes, and helpful information about how to combine prayers for specific ritual purposes.

How this book is organized

Part One is a list of the most common Hebrew prayers used in hospital-type settings. Each prayer is accompanied by its English translation and transliteration.

Part Two is a list of some of the most common Psalms used in these situations.

Part Three is a compilation of some original texts that we have written throughout our work as chaplains. We have also included some insights and instructions for how to write your own prayers.

Part Four is what we call "building blocks" – that is, short verses that can be culled together into longer rituals as you need them.

Part Five is a collection of non-Jewish prayers that you can use for your non-Jewish patients, or adapt for other needs.

Part Six is where we pull it all together for you and offer a few examples of life-cycle rituals which often take place in hospitals. These examples include services for baby-naming, fetal-demise, extubation, and death. You can use the texts we bring here to construct your own services according to the circumstances of your patients.

The Appendices include extra texts and guides for ancillary circumstances and needs.

Appendix A is the Mourner's Kaddish in two different versions – the standard Ashkenazi version that is recited in a quorum, and an ancient Gaonic version that is recited privately by individuals. It is not generally used by chaplains because we do not generally work with prayer quorums. But it is a text tightly associated with death in Jewish tradition, and therefore may be appropriate in certain settings, especially the version available to individuals.

Appendix B is a compilation of blessings for caregivers, often overlooked in chaplaincy. It includes prayers for nurses, night shift workers, and physicians.

Appendix C is a guide for caring for the deceased Jewish patient, helpful instructions for what to do in the immediate aftermath of death.

Finding what you need

Following the Appendix section, we have created several navigational tools to help you find what you need.

We have created an Alphabetical List of Prayers in case you are looking for a specific prayer.

We have also created a standard Index that combines prayers, situations, and topics.

Finally, we created what may be your most important resource in this book: An Index of Events. This table alphabetically lists some of the most common life events that chaplains service in our work. Here, you can scroll through the chart and find your circumstance – e.g., pre-op, birth, death – and find recommendations for texts you can use.

A note on extemporaneous English prayer

Praying in English "from the heart" is a skill in which contemporary Jews, both liberal and traditional, are usually not well-versed. However, this mode of "praying from the heart" is the norm for most Christian patients. It is a skill that is expected of chaplains.

If this is not a skill you currently possess, don't be intimidated. The best advice that we can offer to those attempting extemporaneous prayer in English is this: Pray with honesty, pray with integrity, and keep it short. Don't pretend to be something you are not. Don't pray in a way that is unduly uncomfortable or say things you don't mean. Stay simple, direct, brief, and genuine – and the message will get where it needs to go.

Helpful practices

Here are more tips to make extemporaneous prayer work best for you.

- **Breathe.** Always take a moment to take a deep breath and ground yourself before starting.

- **Decide on a structure for your prayer.** We prefer to use either a three-point prayer or a five-point prayer. More than that is too long.

- **Begin with an invocation.** Call upon Gd in a way that feels comfortable to you. We find that the address "Lord, Gd" or "Ruler of the Universe" translates well, is not strongly gendered, and is usually comfortable for people of different religions with whom we pray.

- **Open with** *"todah"*, **thanks.** Thank Gd for blessings. You may thank Gd for blessings as generic as the new day, or "this moment of prayer" or "the chance to meet and get to

Notes on Style

Transliteration

All Hebrew prayers are brought here in their original, followed by transliteration and translation. The transliterations of Hebrew and Aramaic texts are based on the SBL General Purpose transliteration scheme with slight adaptations.

Version or nusach

For the traditional Jewish prayers, we use the Ashkenazi version of the text as our default text, with apologies for not being able to include all versions throughout. You are invited to make your own adjustments according to your tradition.

Holy Name of Gd

Traditionally, it is believed that we no longer know how to pronounce Gd's name, and even in ancient times it was generally only said in full by the High Priest on Yom Kippur. As such most Jewish people do not pronounce Gd's name and instead say the word Adonai (literally Lord/Master) when reading a prayer out loud, and use the word 'Gd' when speaking about Gd. The name of Gd is seen as something holy and needs utmost respect. In this compendium, we use "Gd" as our preferred English representation of the Holy Name, as well as Adonai and Lord. In the Hebrew text, we include Gd's name, just as other holy books. As such, please treat this volume with the appropriate respect.

Perspective

The prayers vary in terms of speaker perspective. While most prayers can be recited by anyone, some prayers are written in a format meant to be recited by the supplicant, and others by the chaplain on behalf of the supplicant. That is, sometimes the text refers to the ill person as "me" and other times the text uses "he/she". We noted in cases when prayers were specifically written from a particular perspective. That said, the perspective can usually be easily adjusted according to the need at hand with slight language changes, depending on whether the patient wants to pray or to be prayed for.

Gender inclusivity

Hebrew mostly lacks gender-neutral verbs, nouns, and pronouns. We aim to be as gender-inclusive as possible by alternating between male and female forms, sometimes using a slash, such as him/her/them or choleh/cholah. When that becomes cumbersome, we offer separate versions of the prayer for male and female. Resolving the difficult issue of gender neutrality in Hebrew is beyond the scope of this work, but we hope the text offers enough options for you to find respectful solutions for people of all genders.

Lengths of prayers

To make this book easy for a practicing chaplain to use, we included notes about the length of a prayer. "Short" is up to three minutes, "medium" is roughly five minutes, and "long" is seven minutes or more. These are estimates to help you make the best choices for each situation.

Patient's name

Some Hebrew prayers add in the patient's Hebrew name and their mother's Hebrew name. If this is not possible, you can use the person's common name or English name.

Part One:

Top Ten List

In this section, we have collected our ten most-used liturgies. They are cherished traditional prayers that have become standard parts of Jewish liturgy and come in handy in hospitals, hospices, nursing homes, or other healthcare environments. Use them well.

1 Mishebeirach
Traditional Prayer for Healing

Summary	Request for complete healing
Used for	All forms of illness when there is hope for recovery
Length of prayer	Short
Special requirements	Specifically for Jews Traditionally the person's Hebrew name and mother's name are inserted, but the English name also works.
Source	Traditional prayerbook
Original language	Hebrew

This prayer is usually said during communal prayers in synagogue, but a version of it may be appropriate to be used by a chaplain with a single patient. The prayer entreats the Gd of the Patriarchs and Matriarchs to heal the mind, body, and spirit of the ill person.

It is traditional to ask for the Hebrew name of the person being blessed. This small act, asking the person to recall their own Hebrew name, is often a poignant moment in and of itself. It contextualizes the person within a tradition and within a family. The name is usually given to them by their parents and invokes the names of both the parents as a step in naming themselves. Often the Hebrew name is one that older people haven't heard uttered in years, and it can bring back memories of life with their nuclear family. In Ashkenazi culture, people are often named after deceased relatives, and thus the simple act of recalling one's own Hebrew name can evoke the memories and the presence of relatives long gone from this world. Our experience is that people deeply appreciate being asked what their Hebrew name is, and they can get quite emotional when they whisper it to their chaplain. Merely asking for someone's name can create a rich pastoral and ritual moment.

Male

מִי שֶׁבֵּרַךְ אֲבוֹתֵינוּ אַבְרָהָם יִצְחָק וְיַעֲקֹב מֹשֶׁה וְאַהֲרֹן דָּוִד וּשְׁלֹמֹה
וְאִמּוֹתֵינוּ שָׂרָה רִבְקָה רָחֵל וְלֵאָה הוּא יְבָרֵךְ וִירַפֵּא אֶת [פְּלוֹנִי] בֶּן
[פְּלוֹנִית], הַקָּדוֹשׁ בָּרוּךְ הוּא יְמַלֵּא רַחֲמִים עָלָיו לְהַחֲלִימוֹ וּלְרַפֹּאתוֹ
וּלְהַחֲזִיקוֹ וּלְהַחֲיוֹתוֹ, וְיִשְׁלַח לוֹ מְהֵרָה רְפוּאָה שְׁלֵמָה מִן הַשָּׁמַיִם
לְרַמַ"ח אֲבָרָיו וּשְׁסָ"ה גִּידָיו בְּתוֹךְ שְׁאָר חוֹלֵי יִשְׂרָאֵל וְכָל יוֹשְׁבֵי תֵבֵל,
רְפוּאַת הַנֶּפֶשׁ וּרְפוּאַת הַגּוּף, הַשְׁתָּא בַּעֲגָלָא וּבִזְמַן קָרִיב. וְנֹאמַר אָמֵן.

Mi sheberach avoteinu Avraham Yitschak veYa'akov Mosheh ve`Aharon David Ushelomoh Ve'imoteinu Sarah Rivkah Rachel veLe'ah hu yevarech virape et [name of sick individual] ben [mother's name]. Hakadosh baruch hu yimale rachamim 'alav lehachalimo ulerape`oto ulehachaziko ulehachayoto veyishlach lo meherah refu`ah shelemah min hashamayim leramach evarav ushesah gidav betoch she`ar cholei yisra`el vechol yoshvei tevel, refu'at hanefesh urefu`at haguf, hashta ba'agala uvizman kariv. Veno`mar amen.

Female

מִי שֶׁבֵּרַךְ אֲבוֹתֵינוּ אַבְרָהָם יִצְחָק וְיַעֲקֹב מֹשֶׁה וְאַהֲרֹן דָּוִד וּשְׁלֹמֹה
וְאִמּוֹתֵינוּ שָׂרָה רִבְקָה רָחֵל וְלֵאָה הוּא יְבָרֵךְ וִירַפֵּא אֶת [פְּלוֹנִית] בַּת
[פְּלוֹנִית] הַקָּדוֹשׁ בָּרוּךְ הוּא יְמַלֵּא רַחֲמִים עָלֶיהָ לְהַחֲלִימָהּ וּלְרַפֹּאתָהּ
וּלְהַחֲזִיקָהּ וּלְהַחֲיוֹתָהּ, וְיִשְׁלַח לָהּ מְהֵרָה רְפוּאָה שְׁלֵמָה מִן הַשָּׁמַיִם
לְכָל אֵבָרֶיהָ וּלְכָל גִּידֶיהָ בְּתוֹךְ שְׁאָר חוֹלֵי יִשְׂרָאֵל וְכָל יוֹשְׁבֵי תֵבֵל,
רְפוּאַת הַנֶּפֶשׁ וּרְפוּאַת הַגּוּף, הַשְׁתָּא בַּעֲגָלָא וּבִזְמַן קָרִיב. וְנֹאמַר אָמֵן.

Mi sheberach avoteinu Avraham Yitschak veYa'akov Mosheh ve`Aharon David Ushelomoh Ve'imoteinu Sarah Rivkah Rachel veLe'ah hu yevarech virape et [name of sick individual] bat [mother's name] hakadosh baruch hu yimale rachamim 'aleha lehachalimah ulerape`tah ulehachazikah ulehachayotah, veyishlach lah meherah refu`ah shelemah min hashamayim lechol evareha ulechol gideha betoch she`ar cholei yisra`el vechol yoshvei tevel, refu'at hanefesh urefu`at haguf, hashta ba'agala uvizman kariv. Veno`mar amen.

May the One Who blessed our ancestors, patriarchs Abraham, Isaac, and Jacob, matriarchs Sarah, Rebecca, Rachel, and Leah, bless and heal the one who is ill: [name of sick individual] son/daughter of [mother's name]. May the Holy Blessed One overflow with compassion upon him/her, to restore him/her, to heal him/her, to strengthen him/her/them, to enliven him/her/them. The Holy One will send him/her, speedily, complete healing, healing of the soul and healing of the body, along with all the ill, among the people of Israel and all humankind, soon, speedily, without delay, and let us all say: Amen.

2 The Priestly Blessing
An All-Purpose Blessing

Summary	Request for Gd's protection and enlightenment
Used for	Deathbed, recently deceased, compassionate extubation, and various other occasions; It is very adaptable.
Length of prayer	Short
Special requirements	Usually done in Hebrew then in English; can be done with your hands on the person's head (with consent)
Source	Num. 6:24-26
Original language	Hebrew

We use this Biblical blessing to bless nearly all our patients - Baptists, Episcopalians, Catholics, Muslims, Hindus, Jews, and others. People generally love the blessing. A call for Gd's presence and peace seems to have broad appeal, whether the person being blessed is in the hospital or at a bus stop. We bless doctors, taxi-cab drivers, nurses, patients, family members, and the housekeeping staff with these three simple verses.

יְבָרֶכְךָ יְהוָה וְיִשְׁמְרֶךָ.

יָאֵר יְהוָה פָּנָיו אֵלֶיךָ, וִיחֻנֶּךָּ.

יִשָּׂא יְהוָה פָּנָיו אֵלֶיךָ, וְיָשֵׂם לְךָ שָׁלוֹם.

Yevarechcha Adonai veyishmerecha.
Ya`er Adonai panav elecha vichuneka
Yisa` Adonai panav elecha veyasem lecha shalom.

May the Lord bless and protect you.
May the Lord deal kindly and graciously with you.
May the Lord grant you his presence and his peace.

3 Misheberach
for Non-Jews

Summary	Request for Gd's protection and enlightenment
Used for	Deathbed, recently deceased, compassionate extubation, and various other occasions; It is very adaptable.
Length of prayer	Short
Special requirements	Usually done in Hebrew then in English; can be done with your hands on the person's head (with consent)
Source	Num. 6:24-26

This prayer is a contemporary variation of the traditional Jewish Misheberach prayer for healing. Unlike the original, it does not require a Hebrew name to be uttered. Instead of using a Jewish text for the non-Jewish ill person, this prayer speaks to and about the non-Jew. The main divergence from the original is that instead of invoking the "The Gd of Avraham, Isaac, and Jacob" we address this prayer to the "Gd who healed Avimelech and his wife." Of course, we speak of the same one, true Gd, but the address recognizes that the Gd of the Jews healed and continues to heal non-Jews.

Female

מִי שֶׁבֵּרַךְ וְרִפֵּא אֶת אֲבִימֶלֶךְ וְאִשְׁתּוֹ, וְרִפֵּא אֶת כָּל הַדּוֹרוֹת לְפָנָיו וְכָל
צֶאֱצָאָיו, הוּא יְבָרֵךְ וִירַפֵּא אֶת [שֵׁם הַחוֹלֶה] בַּת [שֵׁם הָאִמָּא] שֶׁאָנוּ
מִתְפַּלְלִים עֲבוּרָהּ. הַקָּדוֹשׁ בָּרוּךְ הוּא יִמָּלֵא רַחֲמִים עָלֶיהָ לְהַחֲלִימָהּ
וּלְרַפְּאתָהּ וּלְהַחֲזִיקָהּ וּלְהַחֲיוֹתָהּ, וְיִשְׁלַח לָהּ מְהֵרָה רְפוּאָה שְׁלֵמָה
מִן הַשָּׁמַיִם, רְפוּאַת הַנֶּפֶשׁ וּרְפוּאַת הַגּוּף. וְנֹאמַר אָמֵן.

Mi sheberach veripe et avimelech ve`ishto, veripe` et kol hadorot lefanav vechol tse`etsa`av, hu` yevarech virape` et [name] bat [parent's mother's name] she`anu mitpalelim 'avurah. Hakadosh baruch hu` yimale` rachamim 'aleha lehachalimah ulerape`tah ulehachazikah ulehachayotah, veyishlach lah meherah refu`ah shelemah min hashamayim, refu`at hanefesh urefu`at haguf. Veno`mar amen.

Male

מִי שֶׁבֵּרַךְ וְרִפֵּא אֶת אֲבִימֶלֶךְ וְאִשְׁתּוֹ, וְרִפֵּא אֶת כָּל הַדּוֹרוֹת לְפָנָיו וְכָל צֶאֱצָאָיו, הוּא יְבָרֵךְ וִירַפֵּא אֶת [שֵׁם הַחוֹלֶה] בֶּן [שֵׁם הָאִמָּא] שֶׁאָנוּ מִתְפַּלְלִים עֲבוּרוֹ. הַקָּדוֹשׁ בָּרוּךְ הוּא יְמַלֵּא רַחֲמִים עָלָיו לְהַחֲלִימוֹ וּלְרַפְּאתוֹ וּלְהַחֲזִיקוֹ וּלְהַחֲיוֹתוֹ, וְיִשְׁלַח לוֹ מְהֵרָה רְפוּאָה שְׁלֵמָה מִן הַשָּׁמַיִם, רְפוּאַת הַנֶּפֶשׁ וּרְפוּאַת הַגּוּף. וְנֹאמַר אָמֵן.

Mi sheberach veripe et avimelech ve`ishto, veripe et kol hadorot lefanav vechol tse`etsa`av, hu yevarech virape et [name] ben [parent's name] she`anu mitpalelim 'avuro. Hakadosh baruch hu yimale rachamim 'alav lehachalimo ulerape`oto ulehachaziko ulehachayoto, veyishlach lo meherah refu`ah shelemah min hashamayim, refu`at hanefesh urefu`at haguf. veno`mar amen.

May the Gd who healed Avimelech and his wife and who also healed their ancestors and their children, may He bless and heal him/her/them that stands before us [name of ill person] son/daughter/child of [name of mother/parent(s)] as we pray for him/her/them. Holy One, blessed be your Name, have mercy on him/her/them. Heal and revive him/her/them and send him/her/them a complete recovery, a healing of soul and a healing of body, and let us say: Amen.

know Ms. X." Or you may choose to tailor the thanks more directly to the occasion and the patient you are serving.

- **Continue with** "*bakashot*", **prayers of request.** These are usually tailored to the requests and needs of the patients.

- **Recall your relationships.** Prayer is an opportunity to give voice to what was explored in the visit between chaplain and patient. For example, one might say:

  "Lord, I ask that you bless Ms. Y and her family, protect them and guard them," or: "Lord, we come before you with heavy hearts, which we lift to you. We ask that you help Mr. Z carry the burden of grief that overwhelms him."

- **Finish with Amen.** Finally, close with a rededication of the prayer in the name of the Gd the Creator, the Redeemer, the Healer, etc. And end with "And let us say, Amen."

- **Make space.** You may ask the patient to join you in prayer, or you might begin a prayer and then leave time and room for them to pray independently. Accept that the patient may be praying intentionally or unintentionally to a Gd other than the one you are praying to, or may invoke Jesus.

Whatever you do, pray "*b'lev*", with the heart. Do not recite anything you do not believe or know to be true. Remember that your prayer is an authentic expression of your spirit.

Best of luck in your holy work,

Rabbi M. Chava Evans and Rabbi Eryn London

4 Shalom Aleichem
Come Ministering Angels of Peace

Summary	Welcoming Gd's angels who bring peace
Used for	End of life and extubation
Length of prayer	Medium
Special requirements	Usually sung to a traditional tune; traditionally, each line is recited three times.
Source	Medieval Kabbalists
Original language	Hebrew

The prayer is an entreaty to the ministering Angels of Peace to come and inhabit our space for a while, blessing us as they come. This song is traditionally sung to welcome the Sabbath, but we also use it as an end-of-life prayer. After all, the Sabbath is considered by the sages to represent a taste of the peace and beauty we will enjoy in the world to come. Thus, this seems an appropriate liturgy to use at compassionate extubations or during a deathbed vigil.

There are many tunes for this song, as it has a classic rhythm and is also familiar to many Jews. You can find many popular melodies for Shalom Aleichem on Youtube and elsewhere. When we sing this at a deathbed or extubation, we use the traditional Ashkenazi melody that resembles a lullaby. Each verse may be repeated three times.

שָׁלוֹם עֲלֵיכֶם מַלְאֲכֵי הַשָּׁרֵת מַלְאֲכֵי עֶלְיוֹן

מִמֶּלֶךְ מַלְכֵי הַמְּלָכִים הַקָּדוֹשׁ בָּרוּךְ הוּא.

בּוֹאֲכֶם לְשָׁלוֹם מַלְאֲכֵי הַשָּׁלוֹם מַלְאֲכֵי עֶלְיוֹן

מִמֶּלֶךְ מַלְכֵי הַמְּלָכִים הַקָּדוֹשׁ בָּרוּךְ הוּא.

בָּרְכוּנִי לְשָׁלוֹם מַלְאֲכֵי הַשָּׁלוֹם מַלְאֲכֵי עֶלְיוֹן

מִמֶּלֶךְ מַלְכֵי הַמְּלָכִים הַקָּדוֹשׁ בָּרוּךְ הוּא.

צֵאתְכֶם לְשָׁלוֹם מַלְאֲכֵי הַשָּׁלוֹם מַלְאֲכֵי עֶלְיוֹן

מִמֶּלֶךְ מַלְכֵי הַמְּלָכִים הַקָּדוֹשׁ בָּרוּךְ הוּא.

[נוסח ספרד] בְּשִׁבְתְּכֶם לְשָׁלוֹם מַלְאֲכֵי הַשָּׁלוֹם מַלְאֲכֵי עֶלְיוֹן
מִמֶּלֶךְ מַלְכֵי הַמְּלָכִים הַקָּדוֹשׁ בָּרוּךְ הוּא.
כִּי מַלְאָכָיו יְצַוֶּה לָךְ, לִשְׁמָרְךָ בְּכָל דְּרָכֶיךָ.
יְהֹוָה יִשְׁמֹר צֵאתְךָ וּבוֹאֶךָ, מֵעַתָּה וְעַד עוֹלָם.

Shalom 'aleichem mal`achei hasharet mal`achei 'elyon,
mimelech malchei hamelachim hakadosh baruch hu`.
Bo`achem leshalom mal`achei hashalom mal`achei 'elyon,
mimelech malchei hamelachim hakadosh baruch hu`.
Barechuni leshalom mal`achei hashalom mal`achei 'elyon,
mimelech malchei hamelachim hakadosh baruch hu`.
Tse`techem leshalom mal`achei hashalom mal`achei 'elyon,
mimelech malchei hamelachim hakadosh baruch hu`.
[Sephardic] B'shivtichem leshalom mal`achei hashalom
mal`achei 'elyon, mimelech malchei hamelachim hakadosh
baruch hu`.
Ki mal`achav yetsaveh lach, lishmarecha bechol derachecha.
Adonai yishmor tse`techa uvo`echa, me'atah ve'ad 'olam.

Peace be unto you, ministering angels, messengers of the Most
High, of the supreme King of kings, the Holy One, blessed He.

May your coming be in peace, angels of peace, messengers of
the Most High, of the supreme King of kings, the Holy one,
blessed be He.

Bless me with peace, angels of peace, messengers of the Most
High, of the supreme King of kings, the Holy one, blessed be He.

[Sephardic version] May your return be in peace, angels of peace,
messengers of the Most High, of the supreme King of kings, the
Holy one, blessed be He.

May your departure be in peace, angels of peace, messengers
of the Most High, of the supreme King of kings, the Holy one,
blessed be He.

For He will instruct His angels on your behalf, to guard you in
all your ways. The Lord will guard your going and your coming
from now and for all time.

5 Asher Yatzar
Gd Who Created My Body

Summary	Thank you for creating my body
Used for	Patients with digestive tract issues; before surgery; post-op recovery; going into organ donations.
Length of prayer	Short
Special requirements	Can omit the traditional blessing "formula" at the beginning of the text because we are not fulfilling a mitzvah
Source	Mishnah
Original language	Hebrew

This blessing, colloquially known as the "bathroom blessing", is traditionally recited when a person relieves themselves. It is an extremely significant prayer because it thanks Gd for the very act of allowing our bodies to function. We consider this text a beautiful meditation on the power of everyday bodily performance – how the incapacitation resulting from events such as a gallstone, the blockage of a duct, or the twisting of an intestine can prevent us from being able to approach Gd in prayer. We use this prayer especially for those patients who have gastrointestinal afflictions, and generally to bless all who are ill so that they should, once healed, be able to present themselves comfortably to Gd in prayer.

בָּרוּךְ אַתָּה יְהֹוָה אֱלֹהֵינוּ מֶלֶךְ הָעוֹלָם אֲשֶׁר יָצַר אֶת הָאָדָם בְּחָכְמָה
וּבָרָא בוֹ נְקָבִים נְקָבִים חֲלוּלִים חֲלוּלִים, גָּלוּי וְיָדוּעַ לִפְנֵי כִסֵּא כְבוֹדֶךָ.
שֶׁאִם יִפָּתֵחַ אֶחָד מֵהֶם אוֹ יִסָּתֵם אֶחָד מֵהֶם אִי אֶפְשַׁר לְהִתְקַיֵּם
וְלַעֲמוֹד לְפָנֶיךָ אֲפִילוּ שָׁעָה אֶחָת. בָּרוּךְ אַתָּה יְהֹוָה רוֹפֵא כָל בָּשָׂר
וּמַפְלִיא לַעֲשׂוֹת.

*Baruch atah Adonai eloheinu melech ha'olam, asher yatsar et
ha'adam bechochmah uvara vo nekavim nekavim chalulim chalulim,
galuy veyadua' lifnei kise kevodecha. She`im yipateach echad mehem
o yisatem echad mehem, i efshar lehitkayem vela'amod lefanecha
afilu sha'ah achat. Baruch atah Adonai, rofe chol basar umafli
la'asot.*

King of the Universe, Who formed humanity with wisdom and
created within him openings and hollows, it is obvious and
known in the presence of Your glorious throne that if one of
them were ruptured, or if one of them were blocked, it would
be impossible to exist and stand in Your Presence even for
a short while. Blessed are You, Gd, Who heals all flesh and
performs wonders.

6 Tefillat HaDerech
The Traveler's Prayer

Summary	Request for safety and protection on a journey
Used for	Upon discharge from the hospital or at the end the first interaction if there will be no follow-up
Length of prayer	Short
Special requirements	None
Source	Traditional prayerbook
Original language	Hebrew

This prayer is traditionally said when a Jewish person is traveling from one city to the next. We also find it appropriate to recite on discharge from the hospital. Whenever a patient says, "I'm getting discharged today so I don't need a chaplain," you can offer them a blessing for the road.

יְהִי רָצוֹן מִלְפָנֶיךָ יְהוָה אֱלֹהֵינוּ וֵאלֹהֵי אֲבוֹתֵינוּ, שֶׁתּוֹלִיכֵנוּ לְשָׁלוֹם
וְתַצְעִידֵנוּ לְשָׁלוֹם וְתַדְרִיכֵנוּ לְשָׁלוֹם, וְתַגִּיעֵנוּ לִמְחוֹז חֶפְצֵנוּ לְחַיִּים
וּלְשִׂמְחָה וּלְשָׁלוֹם. וְתַצִּילֵנוּ מִכַּף כָּל אוֹיֵב וְאוֹרֵב וְלִסְטִים וְחַיּוֹת רָעוֹת
בַּדֶּרֶךְ, וּמִכָּל מִינֵי פֻּרְעָנֻיּוֹת הַמִּתְרַגְּשׁוֹת לָבוֹא לָעוֹלָם, וְתִתְּנֵנוּ לְחֵן
וּלְחֶסֶד וּלְרַחֲמִים בְּעֵינֶיךָ וּבְעֵינֵי כָל רֹאֵינוּ, כִּי אֵל שׁוֹמֵעַ תְּפִלָּה וְתַחֲנוּן
אַתָּה. בָּרוּךְ אַתָּה יְהוָה שׁוֹמֵעַ תְּפִלָּה.

Yehi ratson milfanecha Adonai eloheinu ve`lohei avoteinu, shetolichenu leshalom vetats'idenu leshalom vetadrichenu leshalom, vetagi`enu limchoz cheftsenu lechayim ulesimchah uleshalom. Vetatsilenu mikaf kol oyev ve`orev velistim vechayot ra'ot baderech, umikol minei pur'anuyot hamitrageshot lavo la'olam, vetitenenu lechen ulechesed ulerachamim be'einecha uve'einei chol ro`einu, ki el shomea tefilah vetachanun atah. Baruch atah Adonai shomea' tefilah.

May it be Your will, Eternal One, our Gd and the Gd of our ancestors, that You lead us toward peace, support our footsteps towards peace, guide us toward peace, and make us reach our desired destination, for life, joy, and peace. May You rescue us from the hand of every foe, ambush, bandit and wild animal along the way, and from all manner of punishments that assemble to come to Earth. May You send blessing in our every handiwork, and grant us peace, kindness, and mercy in your eyes and in the eyes of all who see us. May You hear the sound of our supplication, because You are the Gd who hears prayer and supplications. Blessed are You, Eternal One, who hears prayer.

7 El Malei Rachamim
Prayer for the Dead

Summary	Praise for compassionate Gd in heaven and request to protect the deceased
Used for	Post-mortem, bed-side, or funerals
Length of prayer	Medium
Special requirements	Chanted in Hebrew in special melody followed by English or brief description. For non-Jews, read only in English.
Source	Traditional prayerbook
Original language	Hebrew

This prayer is usually said at a funeral or memorial service. The (Ashkenazi) melody is hauntingly beautiful.[1] Singing it for a non-Jew might be a bit much, but using the tune as a niggun or wordless, contemplative melody could work quite well.

Jewish tradition has a practice of no prayer between death and the funeral. As such, Jews do not have a liturgy for the recently deceased, by design. After death, in Jewish tradition, all focus is directed towards burying the body with great haste and dignity. Therefore, close relatives of the deceased, upon whom it is incumbent to bury the body, are even discouraged from reciting the daily prayers until they have interred their dead.

Nevertheless, we find that in a hospice or hospital setting this lack of liturgy after death can be confusing, misunderstood, and even hurtful for some people. The mourners often want some Jewish ritual to mark the solemn transition that has just occurred and are left speechless. In a case where there is a body still in the room, and the (Jewish) family is asking for prayer, it is useful to offer options. We will often recite the El Malei Rachamim, which is named for its beginning line, "Gd of compassion."

[1] For a beautiful version sung by Cantor Ariella Forstein "The Songstress Priestess", see: https://www.youtube.com/watch?v=2wth4VQLToc&ab_channel=TheSongstressPriestess

Male

אֵל מָלֵא רַחֲמִים, שׁוֹכֵן בַּמְּרוֹמִים,

הַמְצֵא מְנוּחָה נְכוֹנָה, עַל כַּנְפֵי הַשְּׁכִינָה,

בְּמַעֲלוֹת קְדוֹשִׁים וּטְהוֹרִים, כְּזוֹהַר הָרָקִיעַ מַזְהִירִים,

אֶת נִשְׁמַת [שֵׁם הַנִּפְטָר] בֶּן [שֵׁם הָאִמָּא וְשֵׁם הָאַבָּא] שֶׁהָלַךְ לְעוֹלָמוֹ,

בְּגַן עֵדֶן תְּהֵא מְנוּחָתוֹ.

לָכֵן בַּעַל הָרַחֲמִים יַסְתִּירֵהוּ בְּסֵתֶר כְּנָפָיו לְעוֹלָמִים,

וְיִצְרֹר בִּצְרוֹר הַחַיִּים אֶת נִשְׁמָתוֹ.

יְהֹוָה הוּא נַחֲלָתוֹ,

וְיָנוּחַ בְּשָׁלוֹם עַל מִשְׁכָּבוֹ, וְנֹאמַר אָמֵן.

El male rachamim, shochen bameromim, Hamtse menuchah nechonah, 'al kanfei hashechinah, Bema'alot kedoshim utehorim, kezohar harakia' mazhirim, Et nishmat [name] ben [mother's and father's names] shehalach le'olamo, Began 'eden tehè menuchato. Lachen ba'al harachamim yastirehu beseter kenafav le'olamim, Veyitsror bitsror hachayim et nishmato. Adonai hu nachalato, Veyanuach beshalom 'al mishkavo, venò mar amen.

Female

אֵל מָלֵא רַחֲמִים, שׁוֹכֵן בַּמְּרוֹמִים,

הַמְצֵא מְנוּחָה נְכוֹנָה, עַל כַּנְפֵי הַשְּׁכִינָה,

בְּמַעֲלוֹת קְדוֹשִׁים וּטְהוֹרִים, כְּזוֹהַר הָרָקִיעַ מַזְהִירִים,

אֶת נִשְׁמַת [שֵׁם הַנִּפְטֶרֶת] בַּת [שֵׁם הָאִמָּא וְשֵׁם הָאַבָּא] שֶׁהָלְכָה לְעוֹלָמָהּ.

בְּגַן עֵדֶן תְּהֵא מְנוּחָתָהּ

לָכֵן בַּעַל הָרַחֲמִים יַסְתִּירֶהָ בְּסֵתֶר כְּנָפָיו לְעוֹלָמִים,

וְיִצְרֹר בִּצְרוֹר הַחַיִּים אֶת נִשְׁמָתָהּ.

יְהוָה הוּא נַחֲלָתָהּ,

וְתָנוּחַ בְּשָׁלוֹם עַל מִשְׁכָּבָהּ, וְנֹאמַר אָמֵן.

El male` rachamim, shochen bameromim, Hametse` menuchah nechonah, 'al kanfei hashechinah, Bema'alot kedoshim utehorim, kezohar harakia' mazhirim, Et nishmat [name] bat [mother's and father's names] shehalechah le'olamah Began 'eden tehe` menuchatah. Lachen ba'al harachamim yastireha beseter kenafav le'olamim, Veyitsror bitsror hachayim et nishmatah. Adonai hu` nachalatah, Vetanuach beshalom 'al mishkavah, veno`mar amen.

Gd of compassion, who dwells on high, grant proper repose on the sheltering wings of your presence, in the lofty levels of the holy and pure who shine as the brightness of the firmament, unto the soul of (name of the deceased) child of (father's name and mother's name,) who has gone to his world, and for whose memory we pray. May his repose be in Gd's wings and bind his soul in the bond of life. May the Lord be his heritage, and may he repose on his resting place in peace. And let us say, "Amen."

Vidui
Confession

Summary	Putting affairs in order with Gd and man before death
Used for	Deathbed confession; declaration of faith
Length of prayer	Long (For abridged version, see next entry)
Special requirements	Check with the patient or family that this is a reasonable expression of the person's faith and that this is what they want.
Source	Traditional prayerbook and Yom Kippur
Original language	Hebrew

The Vidui is a traditional confessional prayer recited by, or on behalf of, an individual whose death seems imminent. Many people have an intuitive need for a Jewish form of "last rites" right before death. When that arises, we suggest this prayer, a combination of deathbed confession and declaration of faith, a personal prayer aimed to help people reconcile with Gd and people.

The goal of Vidui is to create a setting that facilitates people's ability to say what they want and need to express at this moment. The text can be adapted in any way you like. It can be recited entirely in English or in combination with the Hebrew, whatever is most comfortable. It is not necessary to do all the sections, and this can be tailored according the family's needs and wishes. You may invite loved ones to add personal thoughts – such as intentions to care for one another, acknowledgment of their relationships, or gratitude for what they shared or learned from each other. In Jewish tradition, authentic words of the heart are always appropriate.

Note that the Vidui does not always mean that death is inevitable at that moment. Many people recite Vidui and then recover. By contrast, if death occurs without Vidui for whatever reason (perhaps it was not possible or appropriate to offer these words before death as the time of death can be unpredictable or chaotic), it is certainly appropriate to offer these words afterward, especially since Jewish tradition teaches that the soul lingers.

Some people may find it helpful to frame this Vidui ritual with a niggun, a wordless melody, as a way of creating sacred time together. They may want to consider Jewish or secular songs that had meaning to their loved one.

The Opening Ritual

The Chaplain's introduction

This Vidui prayer is a marking of a transition from one relationship with Gd to another relationship with Gd – from the relationship with Gd when we're alive to the one we have. The Vidui prayer is also meant to promote peace – peace between people, and peace with Gd.

Breath

Take a moment to focus on your breathing.

Niggun

Open the Vidui ritual with a niggun, a wordless melody, to set the tone and create sacred time together. They may consider Jewish or secular songs that had meaning to their loved one.

Five steps

The following five statements are often a powerful introduction to the Vidui between family members.

I forgive you
Please forgive me
I love you
Thank you
Goodbye

Do these five steps with the family first, and then ask the family to leave so that the person can speak freely. Sometimes people have things to process at death that they do not necessarily want to share with their loved ones. In addition, culturally, we often find that some people do not want to burden their families with this, so it works better if the patient is alone.

The Vidui Texts

Ashamnu Bagadnu

אָשַׁמְנוּ. בָּגַדְנוּ. גָּזַלְנוּ. דִּבַּרְנוּ דֹּפִי. הֶעֱוִינוּ. וְהִרְשַׁעְנוּ. זַדְנוּ. חָמַסְנוּ. טָפַלְנוּ שֶׁקֶר. יָעַצְנוּ רָע. כִּזַּבְנוּ. לַצְנוּ. מָרַדְנוּ. נִאַצְנוּ. סָרַרְנוּ. עָוִינוּ. פָּשַׁעְנוּ. צָרַרְנוּ. קִשִּׁינוּ עֹרֶף. רָשַׁעְנוּ. שִׁחַתְנוּ. תִּעַבְנוּ. תָּעִינוּ. תִּעְתָּעְנוּ.

Ashamenu. Bagadenu. Gazalenu. Dibarenu dofi. He'evinu. Vehirsha'enu. Zadenu. Chamasenu. Tafalenu sheker. Ya'atsenu ra'. Kizavenu. Latsenu. Maradenu. Ni`atsenu. Sararenu. 'Avinu. Pasha'enu. Tsararenu. Kishinu 'oref. Rasha'enu. Shichatenu. Ti'avenu. Ta'inu. Ti'ta'enu.

We have become guilty. We have betrayed. We have robbed. We have spoken slander. We have caused perversion. We have caused wickedness. We have sinned willfully. We have extorted. We have accused falsely. We have given even counsel. We have been deceitful. We have scorned. We have rebelled. We have provoked. We have turned away. We have been perverse. We have acted wantonly. We have persecuted. We have been obstinate. We have been wicked. We have corrupted. We have be abominable, we have strayed, You have let us go astray.

Mode Ani

מוֹדֶה/מוֹדָה אֲנִי לְפָנֶיךָ יְהֹוָה אֱלֹהַי וֵאלֹהֵי אֲבוֹתַי, שֶׁרְפוּאָתִי וּמִיתָתִי בְּיָדֶךָ, עַל כָּל הַחַיִּים וְצָרְכֵי הַחַיִּים שֶׁנָּתַתָּ לִי. יְהִי רָצוֹן מִלְּפָנֶיךָ שֶׁתִּרְפָּאֵנִי רְפוּאָה שְׁלֵמָה. וְאִם אַמּוּת תְּהֵא מִיתָתִי כַּפָּרָה עַל כָּל הַחֲטָאִים וְהָעֲוֹנוֹת וְהַפְּשָׁעִים שֶׁחָטָאתִי וְשֶׁעָוִיתִי וְשֶׁפָּשַׁעְתִּי לְפָנֶךָ. וְתֵן חֶלְקִי בְּגַן עֵדֶן. וְזַכֵּנִי לְעוֹלָם הַבָּא הַצָּפוּן לַצַּדִּיקִים, אֵל נָא רְפָא נָא לִי. אֲנִי מַאֲמִין/מַאֲמִינָה

בֶּאֱמוּנָה שְׁלֵמָה שֶׁאֱלוֹהִים אֱמֶת וּשְׁמוֹ אֱמֶת, וּבִשְׁלֹשָׁה עָשָׂר הָעִקָּרִים. וְהִנְנִי מוֹחֵל/מוֹחֶלֶת לְכָל אָדָם וְהִנְנִי מְבַקֵּשׁ/מְבַקֶּשֶׁת מִכָּל אָדָם לִמְחֹל לִי.

Modeh(m)/modah(f) ani lefanecha Adonai elohay ve`lohei avotay, sherfu`ati umitati beyadecha, 'al kol hachayim vetsarechei hachayim shenatata li. Yehi ratson milefanecha shetirpa`eni refu`ah shelemah. Ve`im amut tehe mitati kaparah 'al kol hachata`im veha'avonot vehapesha'im shechata`ti veshe'aviti veshepasha'ti lefanecha. Veten chelki began 'eden. Vezakeni le'olam haba hatsafon latsadikim, el na refa na li. Ani ma`amin(m)/ma'amina(f) be`emunah shelemah she`elohim emet ushemo emet, uvishloshah 'asar ha'ikarim. Vehineni mochel(m)/mochelet(f) lechol adam vehineni mevakesh(m)/mevakeshet(f) mikol adam limchol li.

I say before you Gd, my Gd and Gd of my forefathers, my healing and my death are in your hands, all of life and necessities of life you have given me. May it be your will that you will heal me, grant me a full healing. If I die, may my death be an atonement for all the sins and wrongdoings that I have erred, sinned, and transgressed before you. Give me a portion in the garden of Eden, and may I merit the World to Come which is concealed for the righteous. Please Gd heal me. I believe with full faith that Gd is true and Gd's name is true, and in the 13 principles of faith. Behold, I forgive everyone and behold I ask that everyone forgives me.

If the above is too difficult to say then one can recite the following:

אִם חַס וְשָׁלוֹם אָמוּת, תְּהֵא מִיתָתִי כַּפָּרָה עַל כָּל עֲוֹנֹתַי.

Im chas veshalom `amut, tehe` mitati kaparah 'al kol 'avonotay

If Gd forbid I die, may my death be atonement for all my wrongdoings.

Mi El Kamocha

During one's final hour, if possible, one should recite the following:

מִי אֵל כָּמוֹךָ נֹשֵׂא עָוֹן וְעֹבֵר עַל פֶּשַׁע לִשְׁאֵרִית נַחֲלָתוֹ לֹא הֶחֱזִיק לָעַד אַפּוֹ כִּי חָפֵץ חֶסֶד הוּא. (מיכה ז;ח)

Mi `el kamocha nose` 'avon ve'over 'al pesha' lish`erit nachalato lo` hechezik la'ad apo ki chafets chesed hu`.

Who, Gd is like you, who forgives wrongdoings and overlooks transgressions for the remnants of His heritage, who has held their anger because He desires kindness. (Micha 7:8)

Beyadecha afkid ruchi

בְּיָדְךָ אַפְקִיד רוּחִי פָּדִיתָה אוֹתִי יְהוָה אֵל אֱמֶת. (תהלים לא:ו)

Beyadecha afkid ruchi paditah oti Adonai el emet.

In Your hand I trust my soul, You redeemed me, Adonai is the Gd of truth. (Psalms 31:6)

Priestly Blessing

יְבָרֶכְךָ יְהוָה וְיִשְׁמְרֶךָ. יָאֵר יְהוָה פָּנָיו אֵלֶיךָ, וִיחֻנֶּךָּ. יִשָּׂא יְהוָה פָּנָיו אֵלֶיךָ, וְיָשֵׂם לְךָ שָׁלוֹם. (במדבר ו;כ"ד-כ"ו)

Yevarechecha Adonai veyishmerecha. Ya`er Adonai panav elecha vichuneka. Yisa` Adonai panav elecha veyasem lecha shalom.

May the Lord bless and protect you. May the Lord deal kindly and graciously with you. May the Lord grant you his presence and peace. (Num. 6:24-26)

Li'yeshu'atech

לִישׁוּעָתְךָ קִוִּיתִי יְהוָה. (בראשית מט:יח)

Li'yeshu'atecha kiviti Adonai.

I long for Your salvation, Gd. (Genesis 49:18)

Adonai El Emet

יְהֹוָה אֵל אֱמֶת, מֹשֶׁה אֱמֶת וְתוֹרָתוֹ אֱמֶת.

Adonai el emet, Moshehmosheh emet vetorato emet.
Gd is the true Gd, Moses is true, and His Torah is true.

Shema

שְׁמַע יִשְׂרָאֵל יְהֹוָה אֱלֹהֵינוּ יְהֹוָה אֶחָד.

Shema yisra`el Adonai eloheinu Adonai echad.
Hear O Israel, Adonai is our Gd, Adonai is one.

בָּרוּךְ שֵׁם כְּבוֹד מַלְכוּתוֹ לְעוֹלָם וָעֶד.

Baruch shem kevod malchuto le'olam va'ed.
Blessed is the Name whose great kingdom is for eternity.

Before passing it is meritorious for one to say or think:

בָּרוּךְ שְׁמוֹ חַי וְקַיָּם לְעוֹלָם וָעֶד.

Baruch shemo chay vekayam le'olam va'ed.
Blessed is His Name, which lives and endures for eternity.

Psalms

Psalms that traditionally are read by those in the presence of someone's final hours:

Psalm 121

שִׁיר לַמַּעֲלוֹת אֶשָּׂא עֵינַי אֶל הֶהָרִים מֵאַיִן יָבֹא עֶזְרִי.

עֶזְרִי מֵעִם יְהֹוָה עֹשֵׂה שָׁמַיִם וָאָרֶץ.

אַל יִתֵּן לַמּוֹט רַגְלֶךָ אַל יָנוּם שֹׁמְרֶךָ.

הִנֵּה לֹא יָנוּם וְלֹא יִישָׁן שׁוֹמֵר יִשְׂרָאֵל.

יְהֹוָה שֹׁמְרֶךָ יְהֹוָה צִלְּךָ עַל יַד יְמִינֶךָ.

יוֹמָם הַשֶּׁמֶשׁ לֹא יַכֶּכָּה וְיָרֵחַ בַּלָּיְלָה.

יְהֹוָה יִשְׁמָרְךָ מִכָּל רָע יִשְׁמֹר אֶת נַפְשֶׁךָ.

יְהֹוָה יִשְׁמָר צֵאתְךָ וּבוֹאֶךָ מֵעַתָּה וְעַד עוֹלָם.

Shir lama'alot esa 'einay el heharim me`ayin yavo 'ezri.

'Ezri me'im Adonai 'oseh shamayim va`arets.

Al yiten lamot raglecha al yanum shomerecha.

Hineh lo yanum velo yishan shomer yisra`el.

Adonai shomerecha Adonai tsilecha 'al yad yeminecha.

Yomam hashemesh lo yakekah veyareach balayelah.

Adonai yishmorcha mikol ra' yishmor et nafshecha.

Adonai yishmor tse`techa uvo`echa me'atah ve'ad 'olam.

A song for ascents. I turn my eyes to the mountains. From where will my help come?

My help comes from the Lord, maker of heaven and earth.

He will not let your foot give way; your guardian will not slumber.

See, the guardian of Israel neither slumbers nor sleeps!

The Lord is your guardian, the Lord is your protection at your right hand.

By day the sun will not strike you, nor the moon by night.

The Lord will guard you from all harm. He will guard your life. The Lord will guard your comings and goings now and forever.

Psalm 130

שִׁיר הַמַּעֲלוֹת מִמַּעֲמַקִּים קְרָאתִיךָ יְהֹוָה.

אֲדֹנָי שִׁמְעָה בְקוֹלִי תִּהְיֶינָה אָזְנֶיךָ קַשֻּׁבוֹת לְקוֹל תַּחֲנוּנָי.

אִם עֲווֹנוֹת תִּשְׁמָר יָהּ אֲדֹנָי מִי יַעֲמֹד.

כִּי עִמְּךָ הַסְּלִיחָה לְמַעַן תִּוָּרֵא.

קִוִּיתִי יְהֹוָה קִוְּתָה נַפְשִׁי וְלִדְבָרוֹ הוֹחָלְתִּי.

נַפְשִׁי לַאדֹנָי מִשֹּׁמְרִים לַבֹּקֶר שֹׁמְרִים לַבֹּקֶר.

יַחֵל יִשְׂרָאֵל אֶל יְהֹוָה כִּי עִם יְהֹוָה הַחֶסֶד וְהַרְבֵּה עִמּוֹ פְדוּת.

וְהוּא יִפְדֶּה אֶת יִשְׂרָאֵל מִכֹּל עֲווֹנֹתָיו.

Shir hama'alot mima'amakim kera`ticha Adonai.

Adonai shim'ah bekoli, tihyenah oznecha kashuvot lekol tachanunay.

Im 'avonot tishmor yah, Adonai mi ya'amod.

Ki 'imecha haselichah lema'an tivare.

Kiviti Adonai kivtah nafshi velidvaro hochaleti.

Nafshi la`donay mishomerim laboker shomerim laboker.

Yachel yisra`el el Adonai ki 'im Adonai hachesed veharbeh 'imo pedut.

Vehu yifdeh et yisra`el mikol 'avonotav.

A song of ascents. Out of the depths I call You, O Lord.

O Lord, listen to my cry. Let your ears pay attention to the sound of my supplications.

If You keep account of sins, O Lord, Lord, how can we bear it?

But you are a forgiving Gd, and for that we feel awe.

I look to the Lord. I look to Him, and I await His word.

I am more eager for the Lord, even more than the night watchman watching for the dawn. Watching for the dawn, O Israel, I wait for Gd. My whole being waits. I wait for Gd's word.

For with the Lord is steadfast love and great power to redeem. It is He who will redeem Israel from all their misdeeds.

Psalm 91

יֹשֵׁב בְּסֵתֶר עֶלְיוֹן בְּצֵל שַׁדַּי יִתְלוֹנָן.

אֹמַר לַיהוָה מַחְסִי וּמְצוּדָתִי אֱלֹהַי אֶבְטַח בּוֹ.

כִּי הוּא יַצִּילְךָ מִפַּח יָקוּשׁ מִדֶּבֶר הַוּוֹת.

בְּאֶבְרָתוֹ יָסֶךְ לָךְ וְתַחַת כְּנָפָיו תֶּחְסֶה צִנָּה וְסֹחֵרָה אֲמִתּוֹ.

לֹא תִירָא מִפַּחַד לָיְלָה מֵחֵץ יָעוּף יוֹמָם.

מִדֶּבֶר בָּאֹפֶל יַהֲלֹךְ מִקֶּטֶב יָשׁוּד צָהֳרָיִם.

יִפֹּל מִצִּדְּךָ אֶלֶף וּרְבָבָה מִימִינֶךָ אֵלֶיךָ לֹא יִגָּשׁ.

רַק בְּעֵינֶיךָ תַבִּיט וְשִׁלֻּמַת רְשָׁעִים תִּרְאֶה.

כִּי אַתָּה יְהֹוָה מַחְסִי עֶלְיוֹן שַׂמְתָּ מְעוֹנֶךָ.

לֹא תְאֻנֶּה אֵלֶיךָ רָעָה וְנֶגַע לֹא יִקְרַב בְּאָהֳלֶךָ.

כִּי מַלְאָכָיו יְצַוֶּה לָּךְ לִשְׁמָרְךָ בְּכָל דְּרָכֶיךָ.

עַל כַּפַּיִם יִשָּׂאוּנְךָ פֶּן תִּגֹּף בָּאֶבֶן רַגְלֶךָ.

עַל שַׁחַל וָפֶתֶן תִּדְרֹךְ תִּרְמֹס כְּפִיר וְתַנִּין.

כִּי בִי חָשַׁק וַאֲפַלְּטֵהוּ אֲשַׂגְּבֵהוּ כִּי יָדַע שְׁמִי.

יִקְרָאֵנִי וְאֶעֱנֵהוּ עִמּוֹ אָנֹכִי בְצָרָה אֲחַלְּצֵהוּ וַאֲכַבְּדֵהוּ.

אֹרֶךְ יָמִים אַשְׂבִּיעֵהוּ וְאַרְאֵהוּ בִּישׁוּעָתִי.

Yoshev beseter 'elyon betsel shaday yitlonan.

Omar la-Adonai machsi umetsudati elohay evtach bo.

Ki hu yatsilecha mipach yakush midever havot.

Be`evrato yasech lach vetachat kenafav techseh tsinah vesocherah amito.

Lo tira mipachad layelah mechets ya'uf yomam.

Midever ba`ofel yahaloch miketev yashud tsohorayim.

Yipol mitsidecha elef urevavah miminecha elecha lo` yigash.

Rak be'einecha tabit veshilumat resha'im tir`eh.

Ki atah Adonai machsi 'elyon samta me'onecha.

Lo te`uneh elecha ra'ah venega' lo yikrav be`oholecha.

Ki mal`achav yetsaveh lach lishmorcha bechol derachecha.

'Al kapayim yisa unecha pen tigof ba`even raglecha.

'Al shachal vafeten tidroch tirmos kefir vetanin.

Ki vi chashak va`afaletehu asagevehu ki yada' shemi.

Yikra`eni ve`e`enehu 'imo anochi vetsarah achaletsehu va`achabedehu.

Orech yamim asbi'ehu ve`ar`ehu bishu'ati.

O you who dwell in the shelter of the Most High and abide in the protection of Shaddai,

I say of the Lord, my refuge and stronghold, my God in whom I trust, that He will save you from the fowler's trap, from the destructive plague.

He will cover you with His wheels; you will find refuge under His wings. His fidelity is an encircling shield.

You need not fear the terror by night, nor the arrow that flies by day, nor the plague that stalks in the darkness, nor the scourge that ravages at noon.

A thousand may fall at your left side, ten thousand at your right, but it shall not reach you.

You will see it with your eyes, you will witness the punishment of the wicked.

Because you took the Lord – my refuge, the Most High – as your haven.

No harm will befall you; no disease shall touch your tent.

For He will order His angels to guard you wherever you go.

They will carry you in their hands lest you hurt your foot on a stone.

You will tread on cubs and vipers. You will trample lions and asps.

Because he is devoted to Me I will deliver him. I will keep him safe, for he knows My name.

When he calls on Me, I will answer him; I will be with him in distress. I will rescue him and make him honored.

I will let him live to a ripe old age, and show him My salvation.

Yigdal

יִגְדַּל אֱלֹהִים חַי וְיִשְׁתַּבַּח, נִמְצָא וְאֵין עֵת אֶל מְצִיאוּתוֹ,
אֶחָד וְאֵין יָחִיד כְּיִחוּדוֹ, נֶעְלָם וְגַם אֵין סוֹף לְאַחְדוּתוֹ.
אֵין לוֹ דְמוּת הַגּוּף וְאֵינוֹ גוּף, לֹא נַעֲרֹךְ אֵלָיו קְדֻשָּׁתוֹ.
קַדְמוֹן לְכָל דָּבָר אֲשֶׁר נִבְרָא, רִאשׁוֹן וְאֵין רֵאשִׁית לְרֵאשִׁיתוֹ.
הִנּוֹ אֲדוֹן עוֹלָם לְכָל נוֹצָר, יוֹרֶה גְדֻלָּתוֹ וּמַלְכוּתוֹ.
שֶׁפַע נְבוּאָתוֹ נְתָנוֹ, אֶל אַנְשֵׁי סְגֻלָּתוֹ וְתִפְאַרְתּוֹ.
לֹא קָם בְּיִשְׂרָאֵל כְּמֹשֶׁה עוֹד, נָבִיא וּמַבִּיט אֶת תְּמוּנָתוֹ.
תּוֹרַת אֱמֶת נָתַן לְעַמּוֹ אֵל, עַל יַד נְבִיאוֹ נֶאֱמַן בֵּיתוֹ.
לֹא יַחֲלִיף הָאֵל וְלֹא יָמִיר דָּתוֹ, לְעוֹלָמִים לְזוּלָתוֹ.
צוֹפֶה וְיוֹדֵעַ סְתָרֵינוּ, מַבִּיט לְסוֹף דָּבָר בְּקַדְמָתוֹ.
גּוֹמֵל לְאִישׁ חֶסֶד כְּמִפְעָלוֹ, נוֹתֵן לְרָשָׁע רָע כְּרִשְׁעָתוֹ.
יִשְׁלַח לְקֵץ הַיָּמִין מְשִׁיחֵנוּ, לִפְדּוֹת מְחַכֵּי קֵץ יְשׁוּעָתוֹ.
מֵתִים יְחַיֶּה אֵל בְּרֹב חַסְדּוֹ, בָּרוּךְ עֲדֵי עַד שֵׁם תְּהִלָּתוֹ.
מֵתִים יְחַיֶּה אֵל בְּרֹב חַסְדּוֹ, בָּרוּךְ עֲדֵי עַד שֵׁם תְּהִלָּתוֹ.

Yigdal elohim chay veyishtabach, nimtsa ve`ein 'et el metsi`uto, Echad ve`ein yachid keyichudo, ne'lam vegam ein sof le`achduto. Ein lo demut haguf ve`eino guf, lo' na'aroch elav kedushato. Kadmon lechol davar asher nivra, ri`shon ve`ein re`shit lere`shito. Hino adon 'olam lechol-notsar, yoreh gedulato umalchuto. Shefa' nevu`ato netano, el anshei segulato vetif`arto. Lo kam beyisra`el keMosheh 'od, navi umabit et temunato. Torat emet natan le'amo el, 'al yad nevi`o ne`eman beito. Lo yachlif ha`el velo yamir dato, le'olamim lezulato. Tsofeh veyodea' setareinu, mabit lesof davar bekadmato. Gomel le`ish chesed kemif'alo, noten lerasha' ra' kerish'ato. Yishlach lekets hayamin meshichenu, lifdot mechakei kets yeshu'ato. Metim yechayeh el berov chasdo, baruch 'adei 'ad shem tehilato. Metim yechayeh el berov chasdo, baruch 'adei 'ad shem tehilato.

Exalted is the living Gd and may Gd be praised. Gd exists and is transcendent. Gd is one and there is no other like Gd. Hidden and infinite is Gd's oneness. Gd has no semblance of a body nor does

Gd have a body. Gd's holiness is not comparable. Gd preceded all that was created. Gd was first and nothing else is first to Gd. Gd is the master of the whole world which Gd created. Gd shows their greatness and majesty. Gd granted prophecy to Gd's splendid people. There has never been another Moses, a prophet who saw his visions clearly. A Torah of truth was given to His people, by the trusted prophet. Gd will never change nor will change Gd's law for eternity. Gd perceives all, is able to see the end at the beginning. Gd rewards kindness according to their deed, and places evil on those who act wickedly. In the End of Days He will send the Messiah, to redeem those waiting for salvation. Gd will revive the dead with all His kindness, blessed be Gd's name forever.

Adon Olam

אֲדוֹן עוֹלָם אֲשֶׁר מָלַךְ, בְּטֶרֶם כָּל יְצִיר נִבְרָא,

לְעֵת נַעֲשָׂה בְחֶפְצוֹ כֹּל, אֲזַי מֶלֶךְ שְׁמוֹ נִקְרָא.

וְאַחֲרֵי כִּכְלוֹת הַכֹּל, לְבַדּוֹ יִמְלֹךְ נוֹרָא,

וְהוּא הָיָה וְהוּא הֹוֶה, וְהוּא יִהְיֶה בְּתִפְאָרָה.

וְהוּא אֶחָד וְאֵין שֵׁנִי, לְהַמְשִׁיל לוֹ לְהַחְבִּירָה,

בְּלִי רֵאשִׁית בְּלִי תַכְלִית, וְלוֹ הָעֹז וְהַמִּשְׂרָה.

וְהוּא אֵלִי וְחַי גּוֹאֲלִי, וְצוּר חֶבְלִי בְּעֵת צָרָה ,

וְהוּא נִסִּי וּמָנוֹס לִי, מְנָת כּוֹסִי בְּיוֹם אֶקְרָא.

בְּיָדוֹ אַפְקִיד רוּחִי, בְּעֵת אִישַׁן וְאָעִירָה,

וְעִם רוּחִי גְּוִיָּתִי, יְהֹוָה לִי וְלֹא אִירָא.

Adon 'olam asher malach, beterem kol yetsir nivra,
Le'et na'asah vecheftso kol, azay melech shemo nikra.
Ve`acharei kichlot hakol, levado yimloch nora,
Vehu hayah, vehu hoveh, vehu yihyeh betif`arah.
Vehu echad ve`ein sheni, lehameshil lo lehachbirah,
Beli re`shit, beli tachlit, velo ha'oz vehamisrah.
Vehu eli vechay go`ali, vetsur chevli be'et tsarah,
Vehu nisi umanos li, menat kosi beyom ekra.
Beyado afkid ruchi, be'et ishan ve`a'irah,
Ve'im ruchi geviyati, Adonai li velo ira.

Master of the Universe, who reigned before all of creation. At the time when all was made by Gd's will, then as King Gd's name was proclaimed. After all ceased to be, alone Gd, the Awesome One, reigned alone. He was He is, He will remain in splendor. Gd is one and there is no other to compare Gd with or to be Gd's equal. With no start and no ending, Gd is the power and dominion. Gd is My Gd, my Redeemer, My Rock in my times of need. Gd is my banner and refuge, the portion in my cup on the day I call. In Gd's hand I entrust my soul, when I go to sleep, I shall awaken. With my spirit I shall remain. Gd is with me, and I will not fear.

Ana Becho'ach

אַנָּא בְּכֹחַ גְּדֻלַּת יְמִינְךָ תַּתִּיר צְרוּרָה.

קַבֵּל רִנַּת עַמְּךָ, שַׂגְּבֵנוּ טַהֲרֵנוּ נוֹרָא.

נָא גִבּוֹר, דּוֹרְשֵׁי יִחוּדְךָ, כְּבָבַת שָׁמְרֵם.

בָּרְכֵם טַהֲרֵם, רַחֲמֵי צִדְקָתְךָ, תָּמִיד גָּמְלֵם.

חֲסִין קָדוֹשׁ, בְּרוֹב טוּבְךָ, נַהֵל עֲדָתֶךָ.

יָחִיד גֵּאֶה, לְעַמְּךָ פְּנֵה, זוֹכְרֵי קְדֻשָּׁתֶךָ.

שַׁוְעָתֵנוּ קַבֵּל, וּשְׁמַע צַעֲקָתֵנוּ, יוֹדֵעַ תַּעֲלֻמוֹת.

בָּרוּךְ שֵׁם כְּבוֹד מַלְכוּתוֹ לְעוֹלָם וָעֶד.

Ana becho'ach gedulat yeminecha tatir tserurah, Kabel rinat 'amecha. Sagevenu taharenu nora. Na gibor, doreshei yichudecha, kevabat shamerem. Barechem taharem, rachamei tsidkatecha, tamid gamelem. Chasin kadosh, berov tuvecha, nahel 'adatecha. Yachid ge`eh, le'amecha peneh, zocherei kedushetecha. Shav'atenu kabel, veshama' tsa'akatenu, yodea' ta'alumot. Baruch shem kevod malchuto le'olam va'ed.

Please will the great strength of Your right hand, untie the tied. Accept the prayer of Your nation; strengthen us, purify us, Awesome One. Please, Strong One, those who seek your oneness, guard them with a watchful eye. Bless them, purify them, have mercy on them, Your righteousness on them for eternity. Powerful Holy One, in all Your goodness, guide your congregation. One and only Exalted one, turn towards Your nation, who are mindful of Your holiness. Accept our pleas and listen to our cries, Knower of hidden thoughts. Blessed is the name whose glorious kingdom is for eternity.

Al Ken

עַל כֵּן נְקַוֶּה לְךָ יְהֹוָה אֱלֹהֵינוּ לִרְאוֹת מְהֵרָה בְּתִפְאֶרֶת עֻזֶּךָ,

לְהַעֲבִיר גִּלּוּלִים מִן הָאָרֶץ וְהָאֱלִילִים כָּרוֹת יִכָּרֵתוּן,

לְתַקֵּן עוֹלָם בְּמַלְכוּת שַׁדַּי וְכָל בְּנֵי בָשָׂר יִקְרְאוּ בִשְׁמֶךָ,

לְהַפְנוֹת אֵלֶיךָ כָּל רִשְׁעֵי אָרֶץ, יַכִּירוּ וְיֵדְעוּ כָּל יוֹשְׁבֵי תֵבֵל,

כִּי לְךָ תִכְרַע כָּל בֶּרֶךְ תִּשָּׁבַע כָּל לָשׁוֹן.

לְפָנֶיךָ יְהֹוָה אֱלֹהֵינוּ יִכְרְעוּ וְיִפֹּלוּ, וְלִכְבוֹד שִׁמְךָ יְקָר יִתֵּנוּ,

וִיקַבְּלוּ כֻלָּם אֶת עֹל מַלְכוּתֶךָ, וְתִמְלֹךְ עֲלֵיהֶם מְהֵרָה לְעוֹלָם וָעֶד.

כִּי הַמַּלְכוּת שֶׁלְּךָ הִיא וּלְעוֹלְמֵי עַד תִּמְלוֹךְ בְּכָבוֹד.

כַּכָּתוּב בְּתוֹרָתֶךָ יְהֹוָה יִמְלֹךְ לְעֹלָם וָעֶד.

וְנֶאֱמַר וְהָיָה יְהֹוָה לְמֶלֶךְ עַל כָּל הָאָרֶץ בַּיּוֹם הַהוּא יִהְיֶה יְהֹוָה אֶחָד וּשְׁמוֹ אֶחָד.

Al ken nekaveh lecha Adonai eloheinu lir`ot meherah betif`eret 'uzecha, Leha'avir gilulim min ha`arets, veha`elilim karot yikaretun, Letaken 'olam bemalchut shaday vechol benei vasar yikre`u vishmecha, Lehafnot elecha kol rish'ei arets, yakiru veyede'u kol yoshevei tevel. Ki lecha tichra' kol berech, tishava' kol lashon. Lefanecha Adonai eloheinu yichre'u veyipolu, velichvod shimcha yekar yitenu, Vikabelu chulam et 'ol malchutecha, vetimloch 'aleihem meherah le'olam va'ed, Ki hamalchut shelecha hi ule'olemei 'ad timloch bechavod. Kakatuv betoratecha, Adonai yimloch le'olam va'ed. Vene`emar vehayah Adonai lemelech 'al kol ha`arets bayom hahu yihyeh Adonai echad ushemo echad.

Therefore, we put hope in you our Gd, that we may soon see your splendor and remove that which is detestable from the earth; That false Gds will be cut out, to fix the world throughout the sovereignty of Shaddai; And all of humankind will call in Your name, and all those who are wicked will turn to You; All the world will know You and bow to You, and all will swear before You Gd; We will fall and bow before you, giving honor to Your name; And all will take the yoke of your kingdom, and You will reign forever; For your Kingdom is Yours and You will reign for eternity in glory, as it says Adonai will reign forever. And as it says, Gd will be king over all of the earth, on that day Gd will be one and Gd's name be one.

The Final Shema

The final Shema verse should be recited by those present immediately prior to passing:

שְׁמַע יִשְׂרָאֵל יְהוָה אֱלֹהֵינוּ יְהוָה אֶחָד.

Shema yisra`el Adonai eloheinu Adonai echad.
Hear O Israel, Adonai is our Gd, Adonai is one.

Recite three times:

בָּרוּךְ שֵׁם כְּבוֹד מַלְכוּתוֹ לְעוֹלָם וָעֶד.

Baruch shem kevod malchuto le'olam va'ed.
Blessed is the Name whose great kingdom is for eternity.

Recite seven times:

יְהוָה הוּא הָאֱלֹהִים.

Adonai hu ha`elohim
Adonai is Gd.

Recite one time:

יְהוָה מֶלֶךְ, יְהוָה מָלָךְ, יְהוָה יִמְלֹךְ לְעוֹלָם וָעֶד.

Adonai melech, Adonai malach, Adonai yimloch le'olam va'ed.
Gd has reigned, Gd reigns, Gd will reign for eternity.

Adonai Natan

After passing, those present recite:

יְהֹוָה נָתַן יְהֹוָה לָקַח. יְהִי שֵׁם יְהֹוָה מְבֹרָךְ. הַצּוּר תָּמִים פָּעֳלוֹ כִּי
כָל דְּרָכָיו מִשְׁפָּט אֵל אֱמוּנָה וְאֵין עָוֶל צַדִּיק וְיָשָׁר הוּא. וְהָלַךְ לְפָנֶיךָ
צִדְקֶךָ כְּבוֹד יְהֹוָה יַאַסְפֶךָ. תִּשְׁכַּב בְּשָׁלוֹם וְתִישַׁן בְּשָׁלוֹם עַד יָבֹא מְנַחֵם
מַשְׁמִיעַ שָׁלוֹם.

*Adonai natan Adonai lakach. Yehi shem Adonai mevorach.
Hatsur tamim po'olo ki kol derachav mishpat el emunah ve`ein
'avel tsadik veyashar hu. Vehalach lefanecha tsidkecha kevod
Adonai ya`asfecha. Tishkav beshalom vetishan beshalom 'ad yavo
menachem mashmia' shalom.*

Gd gives and Gd takes away, may the name of Gd be blessed. The
Rock, perfect is your work, for all Your paths are just, righteous
and fair is He. Your righteous deeds will walk before you, and
the greatness of Gd will gather you. Lay in peace and sleep in
peace, until the arrival of the comforter, the announcer of peace.

Vidui
Abridged

Summary	Putting affairs in order with Gd and man before death
Used for	Deathbed confession; declaration of faith
Length of prayer	Short, or any length
Special requirements	Check that this is a reasonable expression of the person's faith and that this is what they want
Source	Prayerbook and Yom Kippur liturgy
Original language	Hebrew

The traditional Vidui text in the previous entry is long and may not be comfortable for everyone, especially less observant patients who are unaccustomed to that style of prayer. This abridged version is shorter and more interactive. You can find out what parts speak to the person and adapt it according to their needs and interests.

The Opening Ritual

The Chaplain's introduction

The Vidui prayer markes the transition from one relationship with Gd to another relationship with Gd – one we're alive, and another after we've passed. The Vidui prayer is also meant to promote peace – peace between people, and peace with Gd.

Breathe

Please take a moment to focus on your breathing.

Niggun

Let's begin with a niggun, a wordless melody that sets the tone for the moment and helps all focus and enter sacred time.

Chant your niggun

The Vidui Texts

The Chaplain may recite each phrase. The ill person can recite the Vidui and the loved ones who have gathered repeat the phrases addressing each other in turn.

Vidui

אָנָּא, כַּפֶּר לִי עַל כָּל חֲטָאתַי שֶׁחָטָאתִי.

Ana, kaper li 'al koal-chato`tay shechata`ti.

Please forgive me for all the sins that I have sinned.

Additions in English

I'm sorry.

I know that I have made mistakes.

I hope you will forgive me for the times I have disappointed you, hurt you, and angered you.

I know, too, that all human beings make mistakes.

I forgive you.

Abrahamic Blessings

The Chaplain recites:

וַיֹּאמֶר יְהוָה אֶל אַבְרָם לֶךְ לְךָ מֵאַרְצְךָ וּמִמּוֹלַדְתְּךָ וּמִבֵּית אָבִיךָ אֶל
הָאָרֶץ אֲשֶׁר אַרְאֶךָּ.

Vayo`mer Adonai el avram lech lecha mè`artsecha umimoladtecha umibeit avicha el ha`arets asher ar`eka.

Adonai said to Abram, "Go forth from your native land and from your father's house to the land that I will show you.

וְאֶעֶשְׂךָ לְגוֹי גָּדוֹל וַאֲבָרֶכְךָ וַאֲגַדְּלָה שְׁמֶךָ וֶהְיֵה בְּרָכָה.(בראשית י"ב; א-ב)

Ve`e'escha legoy gadol. I will make of you a great nation. Va`avarechcha.

And I shall bless you.

Va`agadelah shemecha.

And I shall make your name great.

Vehyeh berachah.

And you shall be a blessing. (Genesis 12:1-2)

The Chaplain and the patient repeat in turn, addressing those present:

Thank you for the many blessings you have given me, spoken and unspoken. What you have taught me will always remain with me. You are important to me, and you always will be.

Those gathered addressing the patient:

Thank you for the many blessings you have given me, spoken and unspoken. What you have taught me will always remain with me. You are important to me, and you always will be.

The Chaplain and the patient, addressing those present:

Thank you for being the person you are, for loving me. I love you.

Chaplain recites:

וְהוּא אֵלִי וְחַי גּוֹאֲלִי, וְצוּר חֶבְלִי בְּעֵת צָרָה.

Vehu eli vechay goʾali, vetsur chevli beʾet tsarah.

Gd is the source of my life; I turn to Gd in my time of grief.

Those gathered recite:

In grieving I will find resilience. I will miss you, and I will hurt, but I will not be alone.

Final Shema

Chaplain recites:

שְׁמַע יִשְׂרָאֵל יְהֹוָה אֱלֹהֵינוּ יְהֹוָה אֶחָד.

Shemaʾ yisraʾel Adonai eloheinu Adonai echad.

Hear, O Israel, Adonai is our Gd, Adonai is One.

Niggun

Return to the *niggun*, the wordless melody, you began with.

10 Shema
Hear O Israel!

Summary	Declaration of faith for Jews
Used for	Birth, imminent death or capacitation, final moments when a person has the ability to recite this or hear it recited
Length of prayer	Adaptable - short, medium, or long versions
Special requirements	Only appropriate for someone who connects to the faith declaration, not for an atheist or someone who doesn't believe in it
Source	Deuteronomy 6:4-9; Mishnah Yoma 3:8
Original language	Hebrew

The Shema is considered the penultimate Jewish prayer. It is the closest thing that Jews have to a credo. It is meant to be the first prayer a baby hears upon birth and the last prayer a person hears before they die. The text establishes the basic relationship between life and death. It is considered a great kindness to recite these passages to a dying person – but permission should always be asked of the patient or of the family whether it is appropriate. You can recite it with a person or for a person, or they can recite it themselves. Similarly, Shema can be recited for a newborn with permission of the parents.

שְׁמַע יִשְׂרָאֵל יְהוָה אֱלֹהֵינוּ יְהוָה אֶחָד.(דברים ו;ד)

Shema' yisra`el Adonai eloheinu Adonai echad.

Hear, O Israel, Adonai is our Gd, Adonai is One. (Deut 6:4)

בָּרוּךְ שֵׁם כְּבוֹד מַלְכוּתוֹ לְעוֹלָם וָעֶד.

Baruch shem kevod malchuto le'olam va'ed.

Blessed is Gd's glorious majesty forever and ever. (Mishnah Yoma 3:8 inspired by Nechemia 9:5)

וְאָהַבְתָּ אֵת יְהוָה אֱלֹהֶיךָ בְּכָל לְבָבְךָ וּבְכָל נַפְשְׁךָ וּבְכָל מְאֹדֶךָ. וְהָיוּ הַדְּבָרִים הָאֵלֶּה אֲשֶׁר אָנֹכִי מְצַוְּךָ הַיּוֹם עַל לְבָבֶךָ. וְשִׁנַּנְתָּם לְבָנֶיךָ וְדִבַּרְתָּ בָּם בְּשִׁבְתְּךָ בְּבֵיתֶךָ וּבְלֶכְתְּךָ בַדֶּרֶךְ וּבְשָׁכְבְּךָ וּבְקוּמֶךָ. וּקְשַׁרְתָּם לְאוֹת עַל יָדֶךָ וְהָיוּ לְטֹטָפֹת בֵּין עֵינֶיךָ. וּכְתַבְתָּם עַל מְזוּזֹת בֵּיתֶךָ וּבִשְׁעָרֶיךָ. (דברים ו, ו-ט)

Ve`ahavta et Adonai elohecha bechol-levavecha uvechol nafshecha uvechol me`odecha. Vehayu hadevarim ha`eleh asher anochi metsave cha hayom 'al levavecha. Veshinantam levanecha vedibarta bam beshivtecha beveitecha uvelechtecha baderech uveshachebecha uvekumecha. Ukeshartam le`ot 'al yadecha vehayu letotafot bein 'einecha. Uchetavtam 'al mezuzot beitecha uvish'arecha.

You shall love Adonai your Gd with all your heart, with all your soul, and with all your might. Take to heart these instructions with which I charge you this day. Impress them upon your children. Recite them when you stay at home and when you are away, when you lie down and when you get up. Bind them as a sign on your hand and let them serve as a symbol on your forehead. Inscribe them on the doorposts of your house and on your gates. (Deuteronomy 6:5-9)

Notes

Notes

Part Two:

Psalms

You do not have to compose your own prayers. Human beings have been composing prayers for millennia, often around life events that have been common to the human condition then and now. One of the oldest and most diverse collections of these prayers is the Book of Psalms. With 150 texts in which the writers implore Gd regarding issues such as illness, depression, bad relationships, war, hunger, threats of death, and general fears, the Book of Psalms remains a powerful resource for those seeking soulful texts for moments that are spiritually challenging. In fact, much of the Jewish prayerbook is built around texts from Psalms.

In this section, we have collected some of the most poignant and useful chapters that are worth familiarizing yourself with. They speak to pain, longing, reaching out, and calling forth Gd. They speak of Gd as a Healer, Redeemer, Creator, Parent, and King in some of the most eloquent ways ever recorded. You may use them word-for-word or paraphrase sections in extemporaneous prayer. We have also included here some Jewish teachings about these texts.

The sampling of Psalms in this section are the ones we use most frequently. Feel free to use them in any situation and at any time, in Hebrew, English, or any other language. There is never an inappropriate time for the Psalm to be recited.

Learn them. Use them. Love them.

11 Psalm 23: Adonai Ro'i
The Lord is My Shepherd

Summary:	A Psalm expressing faith in Gd, and that even in the darkest of times there is knowledge that Gd is and will be beside them
Used for:	Can be used with someone actively dying or who has just died, or just for general comfort in the face of pain or uncertainty
Length of prayer:	Short
Special requirements:	None
Original language:	Hebrew

This is one of the most familiar and popular Psalms, in both English and Hebrew. It is often recited in times of danger, uncertainty, or fear, and can be used as a Psalm of comfort. Many Jewish people might be familiar with it being sung on Shabbat evening during the third meal.

מִזְמוֹר לְדָוִד: יְהוָה רֹעִי, לֹא אֶחְסָר.

בִּנְאוֹת דֶּשֶׁא, יַרְבִּיצֵנִי; עַל מֵי מְנֻחוֹת יְנַהֲלֵנִי.

נַפְשִׁי יְשׁוֹבֵב; יַנְחֵנִי בְמַעְגְּלֵי צֶדֶק, לְמַעַן שְׁמוֹ.

גַּם כִּי אֵלֵךְ בְּגֵיא צַלְמָוֶת, לֹא אִירָא רָע כִּי אַתָּה עִמָּדִי;

שִׁבְטְךָ וּמִשְׁעַנְתֶּךָ, הֵמָּה יְנַחֲמֻנִי.

תַּעֲרֹךְ לְפָנַי, שֻׁלְחָן נֶגֶד צֹרְרָי.

דִּשַּׁנְתָּ בַשֶּׁמֶן רֹאשִׁי, כּוֹסִי רְוָיָה.

אַךְ, טוֹב וָחֶסֶד יִרְדְּפוּנִי כָּל יְמֵי חַיָּי,

וְשַׁבְתִּי בְּבֵית יְהוָה, לְאֹרֶךְ יָמִים.

Mizmor ledavid: Adonai ro'i, lo echsar.
Bin`ot deshe yarbitseni, 'al mei menuchot yenahaleni.
Nafshi yeshovev, yancheni vema'gelei tsedek, lema'an shemo.
Gam ki elech begei tsalmavet, lo ira` ra' ki atah 'imadi;
Shivtecha umish'antecha, hemah yenachamuni.
Ta'aroch lefanay, shulchan neged tsoreray.
Dishanta vashemen ro`shi, kosi revayah.
Ach tov vachesed yirdefuni kol yemei chayay.
Veshavti beveit Adonai, le`orech yamim.

A Psalm of David. The Lord is my shepherd; I lack nothing.
He makes me lie down in green pastures. He leads me to water
in places of repose.
He renews my life; He guides me in the right paths as befits
His name.
Though I walk through a valley of deepest darkness, I fear no
harm, for You are with me.
Your rod and Your staff – they comfort me.
You spread a table for me in full view of my enemies.
You anoint my head with oil. My cup is full.
Only goodness and steadfast love shall pursue me all the days of
my life.
And I shall dwell in the house of the Lord for many long years.

Reflections on Psalm 23 by Rabbi Eryn

I met C when he was in the family room with his whole family. I am not sure what we started to talk about, but we ended up discussing music and singing. He asked me to sing something.

I sang Psalm 23 in Hebrew to the one tune I could think of. The tune traditionally sung at the third meal towards the end of Shabbat. He told me I should sing that on his deathbed.

I sang Psalm 23 at many more bedsides after that: with a man in the ICU as he was recovering; with a woman as she was dying who had no family – and as I reached the end of the Psalm the doctor pronounced her death; with families who joined in; in the middle of the day and at hours when it was unclear if it was the middle of the night or early morning.

I saw C often after that first visit. Almost a year later unfortunately he was back in the hospital and dying. Somehow it worked out that I was on call that day, that time, and I was called to his room.

I sang with him and his family. Thirty minutes later I heard that he had died.

Psalm 23 went from a song of Shabbat childhood experiences – singing it in my youth group, at synagogue, and at camp – to a song that floods me with memories of patients and feeling the holiness of being with them in those last moments, in moments of comfort and connection.

12 Psalm 40: Kavo Kiviti
I Put my Hope in the Lord

Summary:	Calling out to Gd with the belief that Gd will hear the cry and change the situation at hand
Used for:	Before a big event such as surgery or other procedure
Length of prayer:	Medium
Special requirements:	This might be a difficult Psalm to read if the person does not believe that there is a way out or that Gd has been listening to their prayers. In such circumstances, prayers introducing hope may feel harsh.

This Psalm, which is a call to Gd while in distress, begins with a positive and hopeful note - proclaiming that Gd will be the savior who will destroy the enemies, and that the person praying will receive what they are praying for. Only at the very end is there a sign that the person praying is in distress and unsure of what the outcome will be. It is a potentially painful acknowledgement that perhaps the situation is so big, that the only one who can bring about change is Gd.

Be aware that this Psalm might be a difficult Psalm to read out, as the person we are praying with might not believe that there is a way out or that Gd has been listening to their prayers. Bringing in the idea of hope before the people we are with might feel very harsh to some.

לַמְנַצֵּחַ, לְדָוִד מִזְמוֹר.

קַוֹּה קִוִּיתִי יְהוָה, וַיֵּט אֵלַי, וַיִּשְׁמַע שַׁוְעָתִי.

וַיַּעֲלֵנִי מִבּוֹר שָׁאוֹן מִטִּיט הַיָּוֵן, וַיָּקֶם עַל סֶלַע רַגְלַי, כּוֹנֵן אֲשֻׁרָי.

וַיִּתֵּן בְּפִי שִׁיר חָדָשׁ תְּהִלָּה לֵאלֹהֵינוּ, יִרְאוּ רַבִּים וְיִירָאוּ, וְיִבְטְחוּ, בַּיהוָה.

אַשְׁרֵי הַגֶּבֶר אֲשֶׁר שָׂם יְהוָה מִבְטַחוֹ, וְלֹא פָנָה אֶל רְהָבִים, וְשָׂטֵי כָזָב.

רַבּוֹת עָשִׂיתָ, אַתָּה יְהוָה אֱלֹהַי נִפְלְאֹתֶיךָ וּמַחְשְׁבֹתֶיךָ, אֵלֵינוּ.

אֵין עֲרֹךְ אֵלֶיךָ אַגִּידָה וַאֲדַבֵּרָה, עָצְמוּ מִסַּפֵּר.

זֶבַח וּמִנְחָה לֹא חָפַצְתָּ, אָזְנַיִם כָּרִיתָ לִּי, עוֹלָה וַחֲטָאָה, לֹא שָׁאָלְתָּ.

אָז אָמַרְתִּי, הִנֵּה בָאתִי, בִּמְגִלַּת סֵפֶר, כָּתוּב עָלָי.

לַעֲשׂוֹת רְצוֹנְךָ אֱלֹהַי חָפָצְתִּי וְתוֹרָתְךָ, בְּתוֹךְ מֵעָי.

בִּשַּׂרְתִּי צֶדֶק, בְּקָהָל רָב הִנֵּה שְׂפָתַי, לֹא אֶכְלָא, יְהוָה, אַתָּה יָדָעְתָּ.

צִדְקָתְךָ לֹא כִסִּיתִי, בְּתוֹךְ לִבִּי אֱמוּנָתְךָ וּתְשׁוּעָתְךָ אָמָרְתִּי, לֹא כִחַדְתִּי חַסְדְּךָ וַאֲמִתְּךָ, לְקָהָל רָב.

אַתָּה יְהוָה לֹא תִכְלָא רַחֲמֶיךָ מִמֶּנִּי, חַסְדְּךָ וַאֲמִתְּךָ תָּמִיד יִצְּרוּנִי.

כִּי אָפְפוּ עָלַי רָעוֹת, עַד אֵין מִסְפָּר, הִשִּׂיגוּנִי עֲוֹנֹתַי, וְלֹא יָכֹלְתִּי לִרְאוֹת. עָצְמוּ מִשַּׂעֲרוֹת רֹאשִׁי, וְלִבִּי עֲזָבָנִי.

רְצֵה יְהוָה לְהַצִּילֵנִי, יְהוָה לְעֶזְרָתִי חוּשָׁה.

יֵבֹשׁוּ וְיַחְפְּרוּ יַחַד מְבַקְשֵׁי נַפְשִׁי לִסְפּוֹתָהּ, יִסֹּגוּ אָחוֹר, וְיִכָּלְמוּ, חֲפֵצֵי, רָעָתִי.

יָשֹׁמּוּ, עַל עֵקֶב בָּשְׁתָּם, הָאֹמְרִים לִי, הֶאָח הֶאָח.

יָשִׂישׂוּ וְיִשְׂמְחוּ בְּךָ כָּל מְבַקְשֶׁיךָ, יֹאמְרוּ תָמִיד יִגְדַּל יְהוָה, אֹהֲבֵי, תְּשׁוּעָתֶךָ.

וַאֲנִי עָנִי וְאֶבְיוֹן אֲדֹנָי יַחֲשָׁב לִי, עֶזְרָתִי וּמְפַלְטִי אַתָּה. אֱלֹהַי, אַל תְּאַחַר.

Lamnatseach, ledavid mizmor.

Kavoh kiviti Adonai; vayet elay, vayishma' shav'ati.

Vaya'aleni, mibor sha`on mitit hayaven; vayakem 'al sela' raglay, konen ashuray.

Vayiten befi, shir chadash tehilah lè`loheinu; yir`u rabim veyira`u, veyivtechu, ba'Adonai.

Ashrei hagever asher sam Adonai, mivtacho; velo panah el

rehavim, vesatei chazav.
Rabot 'asita, atah Adonai elohay niflè`otecha
umachshevotecha, eleinu; ein, 'aroch elecha agidah
va`adaberah, 'atsemu, misaper.
Zevach uminchah, lo chafatsta, oznayim karita li; 'olah
vachatà`ah, lo shà`aleta.
Az amarti, hineh và`ti; bimgilat sefer, katuv 'alay.
La'asot retsonecha elohay chafatseti vetoratecha, betoch me'ay.
Bisarti tsedek, bekahal rav hineh sefatay, lo echlà; Adonai,
atah yada'eta.
Tsidkatecha lo chisiti, betoch libi, emunatecha uteshu'atecha
amareti; lo chichadti chasdecha và`amitecha, lekahal rav.
Atah Adonai lo tichla rachamecha mimeni; chasdecha
và`amitecha, tamid yitseruni.
Ki afefu 'alay ra'ot, 'ad ein mispar, hisiguni 'avonotay, velo
yacholeti lir`ot; 'atsemu misa'arot rò`shi, libi 'azavani.
Retseh Adonai, lehatsileni; Adonai, le'ezrati chushah.
Yevoshu veyachperu yachad, mevakshei nafshi, lispotah;
yisogu achor, veyikalmu, chafetsei, ra'ati.
Yashomu, 'al 'ekev boshtam, hà`omerim li, he`ach he`ach.
Yasisu veyismechu, becha kal-mevakshecha; yò`meru tamid,
yigdal Adonai, ohavei, teshu'atecha.
Và`ani, 'ani vè`evyon Adonai yachashav li. 'Ezrati umefalti
atah; elohay, al-tè`achar.

For the victor, a Psalm of David.
I put my hope in the Lord; He inclined toward me and heeded my cry.
He lifted me out of the miry pit, the slimy clay, and set my feet on a rock, steadied my legs.
He put a new song into my mouth, a hymn to our God. May many see it and stand in awe, and trust in the Lord.

Happy is the man who makes the Lord his trust, who turns not to the arrogant or to followers of falsehood.

You, O Lord my God, have done many things. The wonders You have devised for us cannot be set out before You. I would rehearse the tale of them, but they are more than can be told. You enabled me to understand that. You do not desire sacrifice and meal offering; You do not ask for burnt offering and sin offering.

Then I said, "See, I will bring a scroll recounting what befell me." To do what pleases You, my God, is my desire. Your teaching is in my inmost parts.

I proclaimed [Your] righteousness in a great congregation. See, I did not withhold my words. O Lord, You must know it.

I did not keep Your beneficence to myself. I declared Your faithful deliverance. I did not fail to speak of Your steadfast love in a great congregation.

O Lord, You will not withhold from me Your compassion. Your steadfast love will protect me always.

For misfortunes without number envelop me. My iniquities have caught up with me. I cannot see for they are more than the hairs of my head. I am at my wits' end.

O favor me, Lord, and save me. O Lord, hasten to my aid. Let those who seek to destroy my life be frustrated and disgraced. Let those who wish me harm fall back in shame. Let those who say "Aha! Aha!" over me be desolate because of their frustration.

But let all who seek You be glad and rejoice in You. Let those who are eager for Your deliverance always say, "Extolled be the Lord!"

But I am poor and needy. May the Lord devise [deliverance] for me. You are my help and my rescuer. My God, do not delay.

13 Psalm 63: Tzam'a Nafshi
My Soul Thirsts for You

Summary:	The Psalmist is in distress but believes that no matter what, they can reach out to Gd – and Gd will be there for them.
Used for:	Can be used at a difficult or scary period, perhaps when the patient or family express feeling "abandoned" by Gd, while at the same time speaking about faith in Gd.
Length of prayer:	Medium
Special requirements:	None

The Psalm opens with the idea of being in a spiritual "desert" and "thirsting for Gd". The Psalmist powerfully describes feeling alone, lost, and perhaps close to death, but nevertheless believes that even at this most difficult moment, Gd has not abandoned them in their time of need.

מִזְמוֹר לְדָוִד בִּהְיוֹתוֹ בְּמִדְבַּר יְהוּדָה.

אֱלֹהִים אֵלִי אַתָּה אֲשַׁחֲרֶךָּ צָמְאָה לְךָ נַפְשִׁי כָּמַהּ לְךָ בְשָׂרִי בְּאֶרֶץ צִיָּה וְעָיֵף בְּלִי מָיִם.

כֵּן בַּקֹּדֶשׁ חֲזִיתִךָ לִרְאוֹת עֻזְּךָ וּכְבוֹדֶךָ.

כִּי טוֹב חַסְדְּךָ מֵחַיִּים שְׂפָתַי יְשַׁבְּחוּנְךָ.

כֵּן אֲבָרֶכְךָ בְחַיָּי בְּשִׁמְךָ אֶשָּׂא כַפָּי.

כְּמוֹ חֵלֶב וָדֶשֶׁן תִּשְׂבַּע נַפְשִׁי וְשִׂפְתֵי רְנָנוֹת יְהַלֶּל פִּי.

אִם זְכַרְתִּיךָ עַל יְצוּעָי בְּאַשְׁמֻרוֹת אֶהְגֶּה בָּךְ.

כִּי הָיִיתָ עֶזְרָתָה לִּי וּבְצֵל כְּנָפֶיךָ אֲרַנֵּן.

דָּבְקָה נַפְשִׁי אַחֲרֶיךָ בִּי תָּמְכָה יְמִינֶךָ.

וְהֵמָּה לְשׁוֹאָה יְבַקְשׁוּ נַפְשִׁי יָבֹאוּ בְּתַחְתִּיּוֹת הָאָרֶץ.

יַגִּירֻהוּ עַל יְדֵי חָרֶב מְנָת שֻׁעָלִים יִהְיוּ.

וְהַמֶּלֶךְ יִשְׂמַח בֵּאלֹהִים יִתְהַלֵּל כָּל הַנִּשְׁבָּע בּוֹ כִּי יִסָּכֵר פִּי דוֹבְרֵי שָׁקֶר.

Mizmor ledavid bihyoto bemidbar yehudah.
Elohim eli atah ashachareka tsame`ah lecha nafshi kamah lecha
besari be`erets tsiyah ve'ayef beli-mayim.
Ken bakodesh chaziticha lir`ot 'uzecha uchevodecha.
Ki tov chasdecha mechayim sefatay yeshabechunecha.
Ken avarechecha vechayay beshimcha esa chapay.
Kemo chelev vadeshen tisba' nafshi vesiftei renanot yehalel pi.
Im zecharticha 'al yetsu'ay be`ashmurot ehgeh bach.
Ki hayita 'ezratah li uvetsel kenafecha aranen.
Davekah nafshi acharecha bi tamechah yeminecha.
Vehemah lesho`ah yevakshu nafshi yavo`u betachtiyot ha`arets.
Yagiruhu 'al yedei charev menat shu'alim yihyu.
Vehamelech yismach be`lohim yithalel kol hanishba' bo ki
yisacher pi doverei shaker.

A Psalm of David, when he was in the wilderness of Judah.

God, You are my God; I search for You, my soul thirsts for You, my body yearns for You, as a parched and thirsty land that has no water.

I shall behold You in the sanctuary, and see Your might and glory,

Truly Your faithfulness is better than life; my lips declare Your praise.

I bless You all my life; I lift up my hands, invoking Your name.

I am sated as with a rich feast; I sing praises with joyful lips.

When I call You to mind upon my bed, when I think of You in the watches of the night.

For You are my help, and in the shadow of Your wings I shout for joy.

My soul is attached to You; Your right hand supports me.

May those who seek to destroy my life enter the depths of the earth.

May they be gutted by the sword; may they be prey to jackals.

But the king shall rejoice in God; all who swear by Him shall exult, when the mouth of liars is stopped.

14 Psalm 91: Yoshev b'Seter
You who Dwell

Summary:	Reflections on being "under the wings of Gd"
Used for:	Right before or after death; To offer comfort to someone who is in distress.
Length of prayer:	Medium
Special requirements:	None

This Psalm describes feeling safe, protected, and "under the wings of Gd." This is a place of feeling close to Gd. It is an appropriate Psalm to recite for those in distress, or right before or after death.

יֹשֵׁב בְּסֵתֶר עֶלְיוֹן בְּצֵל שַׁדַּי יִתְלוֹנָן.

אֹמַר לַיהוָֹה מַחְסִי וּמְצוּדָתִי אֱלֹהַי אֶבְטַח בּוֹ.

כִּי הוּא יַצִּילְךָ מִפַּח יָקוּשׁ מִדֶּבֶר הַוּוֹת.

בְּאֶבְרָתוֹ יָסֶךְ לָךְ וְתַחַת כְּנָפָיו תֶּחְסֶה צִנָּה וְסֹחֵרָה אֲמִתּוֹ.

לֹא תִירָא מִפַּחַד לָיְלָה מֵחֵץ יָעוּף יוֹמָם.

מִדֶּבֶר בָּאֹפֶל יַהֲלֹךְ מִקֶּטֶב יָשׁוּד צָהֳרָיִם.

יִפֹּל מִצִּדְּךָ אֶלֶף וּרְבָבָה מִימִינֶךָ אֵלֶיךָ לֹא יִגָּשׁ.

רַק בְּעֵינֶיךָ תַבִּיט וְשִׁלֻּמַת רְשָׁעִים תִּרְאֶה.

כִּי אַתָּה יְהוָֹה מַחְסִי עֶלְיוֹן שַׂמְתָּ מְעוֹנֶךָ.

לֹא תְאֻנֶּה אֵלֶיךָ רָעָה וְנֶגַע לֹא יִקְרַב בְּאָהֳלֶךָ.

כִּי מַלְאָכָיו יְצַוֶּה לָּךְ לִשְׁמָרְךָ בְּכָל דְּרָכֶיךָ.

עַל כַּפַּיִם יִשָּׂאוּנְךָ פֶּן תִּגֹּף בָּאֶבֶן רַגְלֶךָ.

עַל שַׁחַל וָפֶתֶן תִּדְרֹךְ תִּרְמֹס כְּפִיר וְתַנִּין.

כִּי בִי חָשַׁק וַאֲפַלְּטֵהוּ אֲשַׂגְּבֵהוּ כִּי יָדַע שְׁמִי.

יִקְרָאֵנִי וְאֶעֱנֵהוּ עִמּוֹ אָנֹכִי בְצָרָה אֲחַלְּצֵהוּ וַאֲכַבְּדֵהוּ.

אֹרֶךְ יָמִים אַשְׂבִּיעֵהוּ וְאַרְאֵהוּ בִּישׁוּעָתִי.

Yoshev beseter 'elyon betsel shaday yitlonan.
Omar la-Adonai machsi umetsudati elohay evtach bo.
Ki hu yatsilecha mipach yakush midever havot.
Be`evrato yasech lach vetachat kenafav techseh tsinah
vesocherah amito.
Lo tira mipachad layelah mechets ya'uf yomam.
Midever ba`ofel yahaloch miketev yashud tsohorayim.
Yipol mitsidecha elef urevavah miminecha elecha lo` yigash.
Rak be'einecha tabit veshilumat resha'im tir`eh.
Ki atah Adonai machsi 'elyon samta me'onecha.
Lo te`uneh elecha ra'ah venega' lo yikrav be`oholecha.
Ki mal`achav yetsaveh lach lishmorcha bechol derachecha.
'Al kapayim yisa unecha pen tigof ba`even raglecha.
'Al shachal vafeten tidroch tirmos kefir vetanin.
Ki vi chashak va`afaletehu asagevehu ki yada' shemi.
Yikra`eni ve`e'enehu 'imo anochi vetsarah achaletsehu
va`achabedehu.
Orech yamim asbi'ehu ve`ar`ehu bishu'ati.

O you who dwell in the shelter of the Most High and abide in the protection of Shaddai,

I say of the Lord, my refuge and stronghold, my God in whom I trust, that He will save you from the fowler's trap, from the destructive plague.

He will cover you with His wheels; you will find refuge under His wings. His fidelity is an encircling shield.

You need not fear the terror by night, nor the arrow that flies by day, nor the plague that stalks in the darkness, nor the scourge that ravages at noon.

A thousand may fall at your left side, ten thousand at your right, but it shall not reach you.

You will see it with your eyes, you will witness the punishment of the wicked.

Because you took the Lord – my refuge, the Most High – as your haven.

No harm will befall you; no disease shall touch your tent.

For He will order His angels to guard you wherever you go.

They will carry you in their hands lest you hurt your foot on a stone.

You will tread on cubs and vipers. You will trample lions and asps.

Because he is devoted to Me I will deliver him. I will keep him safe, for he knows My name.

When he calls on Me, I will answer him; I will be with him in distress. I will rescue him and make him honored.

I will let him live to a ripe old age, and show him My salvation.

15 Psalm 121
Esa Einai, I will Lift Up My Eyes to the Hills

Summary:	An exclamation of certainty that Gd will be with them and protect them in their time of need
Used for:	Before surgery or a procedure, or while awaiting news of a diagnosis and prognosis.
Length of prayer:	Short
Special requirements:	None

This classic text offers comfort during anxious moments of uncertainty. It is often said before a surgery or procedure, or while awaiting news of a diagnosis and prognosis. Excerpts from this Psalm may be helpful in formulating prayer language in English. The Psalm has also been set to music and some lovely versions are available on Youtube and elsewhere.[1]

---

[1] See, for example, a soulful musical version by the Maayan Band https://www.youtube.com/watch?v=3BculQjG_Oo&ab_channel=MaayanBand

שִׁיר לַמַּעֲלוֹת אֶשָּׂא עֵינַי אֶל הֶהָרִים מֵאַיִן יָבֹא עֶזְרִי.
עֶזְרִי מֵעִם יְהֹוָה עֹשֵׂה שָׁמַיִם וָאָרֶץ.
אַל יִתֵּן לַמּוֹט רַגְלֶךָ אַל יָנוּם שֹׁמְרֶךָ.
הִנֵּה לֹא יָנוּם וְלֹא יִישָׁן שׁוֹמֵר יִשְׂרָאֵל.
יְהֹוָה שֹׁמְרֶךָ יְהֹוָה צִלְּךָ עַל יַד יְמִינֶךָ.
יוֹמָם הַשֶּׁמֶשׁ לֹא יַכֶּכָּה וְיָרֵחַ בַּלָּיְלָה.
יְהֹוָה יִשְׁמָרְךָ מִכָּל רָע יִשְׁמֹר אֶת נַפְשֶׁךָ.
יְהֹוָה יִשְׁמָר צֵאתְךָ וּבוֹאֶךָ מֵעַתָּה וְעַד עוֹלָם.

Shir lama'alot esa 'einay el heharim me`ayin yavo 'ezri.
'Ezri me'im Adonai 'oseh shamayim va`arets.
Al yiten lamot raglecha al yanum shomerecha.
Hineh lo yanum velo yishan shomer yisra`el.
Adonai shomerecha Adonai tsilecha 'al yad yeminecha.
Yomam hashemesh lo yakekah veyareach balayelah.
Adonai yishmorcha mikol ra' yishmor et nafshecha.
Adonai yishmor tse`techa uvo`echa me'atah ve'ad 'olam.

A song for ascents. I turn my eyes to the mountains. From where will my help come?

My help comes from the Lord, maker of heaven and earth.

He will not let your foot give way; your guardian will not slumber.

See, the guardian of Israel neither slumbers nor sleeps!

The Lord is your guardian, the Lord is your protection at your right hand.

By day the sun will not strike you, nor the moon by night.

The Lord will guard you from all harm. He will guard your life.

The Lord will guard your comings and goings now and forever.

16 Psalm 130: Mima'amakim
From the Depths I Call to You

Summary:	A call to Gd from a place of despair, with certainty that Gd will respond
Used for:	Moments of inner torment. Validates that one can cry, or be upset and even angry with Gd in a moment of great pain, while still maintaining faith.
Length of prayer:	Short
Special requirements:	None

This Psalm expresses great anguish and is helpful for people experiencing severe pain or torment. It is especially useful when working with people of faith (Jewish, Christian, or other) who are feeling distressed, but experience guilt or shame because they believe that they are not allowed to feel that way. The Psalm is a reminder that even King David felt pain, and in his suffering called out to Gd – and that we, too, can therefore use his words to call out to Gd in our time of agony.

The Psalm in its entirety is probably best suited for a Jewish patient, but excerpts are certainly appropriate to all who wait for Gd's word.

שִׁיר הַמַּעֲלוֹת מִמַּעֲמַקִּים קְרָאתִיךָ יְהֹוָה.

אֲדֹנָי שִׁמְעָה בְקוֹלִי תִּהְיֶינָה אָזְנֶיךָ קַשֻּׁבוֹת לְקוֹל תַּחֲנוּנָי.

אִם עֲוֹנוֹת תִּשְׁמָר יָהּ אֲדֹנָי מִי יַעֲמֹד.

כִּי עִמְּךָ הַסְּלִיחָה לְמַעַן תִּוָּרֵא.

קִוִּיתִי יְהֹוָה קִוְּתָה נַפְשִׁי וְלִדְבָרוֹ הוֹחָלְתִּי.

נַפְשִׁי לַאדֹנָי מִשֹּׁמְרִים לַבֹּקֶר שֹׁמְרִים לַבֹּקֶר.

יַחֵל יִשְׂרָאֵל אֶל יְהֹוָה כִּי עִם יְהֹוָה הַחֶסֶד וְהַרְבֵּה עִמּוֹ פְדוּת.

וְהוּא יִפְדֶּה אֶת יִשְׂרָאֵל מִכֹּל עֲוֹנֹתָיו.

Shir hama'alot mima'amakim kera`ticha Adonai.
Adonai shim'ah bekoli, tihyenah oznecha kashuvot lekol tachanunay.
Im 'avonot tishmor yah, Adonai mi ya'amod.
Ki 'imecha haselichah lema'an tivare.
Kiviti Adonai kivtah nafshi velidvaro hochaleti.
Nafshi la`donay mishomerim laboker shomerim laboker.
Yachel yisra`el el Adonai ki 'im Adonai hachesed veharbeh 'imo pedut.
Vehu yifdeh et yisra`el mikol 'avonotav.

A song of ascents. Out of the depths I call You, O Lord.

O Lord, listen to my cry. Let your ears pay attention to the sound of my supplications.

If You keep account of sins, O Lord, Lord, how can we bear it?

But you are a forgiving Gd, and for that we feel awe.

I look to the Lord. I look to Him, and I await His word.

I am more eager for the Lord, even more than the night watchman watching for the dawn. Watching for the dawn, O Israel, I wait for Gd. My whole being waits. I wait for Gd's word.

For with the Lord is steadfast love and great power to redeem. It is He who will redeem Israel from all their misdeeds.

Reflections on Psalm 130 by Rabbi M. Chava

Hospitals are full of people waiting. In one room a patient awaits a liver transplant. In another unit, a father waits for his wife to give birth. Down the hall, a patient waits for her seven days of chemo to be over. In room eight, someone is waiting for a prescription to be filled. In room ten, they wait for the results of a biopsy. One man waits for his numbers to go up; another waits for his numbers to go down. There's so much anxiety. So much time passes as we remain suspended in limbo, in the nowhere of waiting, in the space in between certainties.

In each of the above scenarios, the person is waiting for some action. Some of us might suggest that they are waiting on the Holy One to act or to speak. And although somewhere deep down, a part of us might remember that time runs as the Creator wills it, not as we want, we nevertheless, continue to be anxious.

Psalm 130 is all about waiting for Gd. We read: "Even more than the night watchman, watching for the dawn, I wait for Gd [to act]. My whole being waits. I wait for Gd's word." In my faith tradition, the Jewish tradition, this passage speaks of the Israelites waiting on Gd to redeem them from exile. Earlier, we read, "By the rivers of Babylon, we sat down, and we wept, and we remembered Zion." They are waiting for a return to their homeland.

As the Israelite waits, so each of us at one time or another inhabits that unsettling period —before the doctor arrives, before the meds kick in, before the pain stops. Waiting for Gd to act can feel as though we are waiting for Gd Gd's self. But let us be reminded: waiting on the Holy One's *action* and waiting on the Holy One's *presence* are two different things.

Gd is with us in the surgery waiting room, as we drink our second predawn cup of coffee, in the cafeteria at eight at night, and in the ER waiting room at midnight. In the Intensive care unit, Gd waits with us amidst the cacophony of beeps and alarms. Gd's word may not be revealed yet, but Gd is there even before He grants us word, knowledge, or deed.

In the book of Job, each of Job's friends bring a different answer to the question of why Job is suffering. But none of his friends' explanations and answers bring Job any comfort. Ultimately, only the awesome presence of the Holy One brings comfort to Job. "My whole being waits. I wait for Gd's word." Somewhat paradoxically, we wait for Gd's words with Gd's presence beside us. Answers and results may, in the material word, bring great comfort or they may bring great distress. The ever-present Holy One always brings comfort, despite the content of these answers or results.

Each of us has the opportunity to act in the image of the Divine by being present to others as they wait. We must always attempt to be present to uncertainty, ambiguity, or mystery.

As we say in the Jewish tradition, "Have courage and hope in the Lord."

Let us pray.
My soul waits for the Lord.
Holy One, we commend to your faithful love
Those who are crying out from the depths.
Help us and them to watch and pray
Through their time of darkness
In sure hope of dawn

Notes

Part Three:

Original Texts

Jews do not have a strong tradition of praying "off the cuff" or in English. But through our chaplaincy, we have come to appreciate spontaneous, extemporaneous personal prayers. We found there is often a need to pray in English in a way that sounds natural, heartfelt, and resonant with both Jewish and non-Jewish patients. As we familiarized ourselves with prayer books from a variety of faith traditions, we learned how to use prayer to highlight the meanings of our interactions and exchanges with people. Most importantly, we came to understand that prayer can be a product of listening to the other and reflecting back what you have heard with the intent of lifting them towards the Divine.

Over the years, we have had many opportunities to create original prayers in response to situations that we faced. We have come to enjoy not only our scripted traditions but also these custom-crafted supplications. We see this as a positive, creative, and compassionate approach to our work. We encourage you to do the same.

In this section, we present some of the texts we have written over the years that you may find helpful.

17 One-Handed Prayer

Summary:	Short, pointed prayers about anything on people's minds
Used for:	Anything, especially a specific need
Length of prayer:	Short
Special requirements:	None
Author:	Rabbi M. Chava Evans
Original Language:	English

Reflections from Rabbi M. Chava

When I pray in English extemporaneously, I often follow a formula in which I create a prayer with sections that I can count out on the fingers of one hand. That is my rule, because anything longer than five parts is, I think, unnecessary. My prayers often have a beginning, a middle and an end. Often I ask for 1-4 blessings for the assembled based on what they have told me about their situation. I call these my "One Handed Prayers" because I think of the parts beforehand and then I tap my finger surreptitiously each time I begin a new section.

Below is a prayer that I wrote for a Baptist family one late evening at the bedside of a patient who was going for a procedure in the morning and whose adult son and sister drove through the night in order to be at the patient's bedside. The patient told me he was struggling to keep his faith. So, I wrote this version of my One-Handed Prayer, a very straightforward, unpretentious prayer that was well received.

One-Handed Prayer: A Bedside Prayer for a Baptist Patient

Gracious and Heavenly Father,

I want to thank you for this moment of prayer that I share with [name of patient]. For in prayer, we can center ourselves in Your Peace and in Your Presence. We affirm that You are the Source of all blessings and that nothing is too great for You. For the blessings we have received, Lord, make us truly grateful. [Feel free to add more specifics here.] I humbly ask that you continue to shower blessings upon [name of patient]. In particular Lord, I want to ask for four blessings for this family.

Firstly, I want to ask for Your blessings of *peace*. Let this family walk together, arm in arm as they are now, one step at a time with their feet firm and their heads held high. One step at a time, Lord, and I say to them, "Don't look down." Just keep your senses in the present and trust in you. Grant them peace and discernment as they attempt to reconcile themselves to your will. You didn't bring them this far to drop them.

Secondly, Lord, I want to ask for your blessing of *strength* upon them. They are weary and they need you to help lift their spirits and their bodies. Let them sleep well tonight, knowing that [name of patient] is in good hands and let [name of patient] sleep well tonight, knowing that he is safe. Blessed are you Lord, who gives strength to the weary.

Thirdly, Lord, I want to ask for Your blessing of *love* upon this family. Let them know that they are loved by you with a Great Love. Let them feel your love. Grant them the tools they require, Lord, to be loving to one another and to lift one another up through this illness. And Lord, grant them faith in you, which is a kind of Love.

And finally, Lord, I ask for the blessing of *healing*. I ask for healing for [name of patient] as well as for his sister [name], his son [name] and all their loved ones, a healing of body, mind, and soul, and a healing of faith. You know better than anyone the ways in which we need to be healed. You are the great Healer and we call out to You and put our trust in You.

For all these blessings, Lord, and for the prayers of our heart which remain unspoken, I humbly ask for your consideration.

And let us all say, Amen.

18 Balms

Summary:	A direct appeal to Gd that our spiritual needs should be fulfilled
Used for:	Occasions that are particularly emotionally raw
Length of prayer:	Short
Special requirements:	None
Author:	Rabbi M. Chava Evans
Original Language:	English

This short prayer goes to the place of emotional and spiritual exhaustion. It can be used when someone is in great pain or distress and there is nothing else to say.

Gd, grant mercy to my imperfect soul.

Gd, grant strength to my tired soul.

Gd, grant peace to my anxious soul.

Gd, grant healing to my ill soul.

Gd, grant comfort to my suffering soul.

Gd, grant mending to my frayed soul.

Gd, grant love to my lonely soul.

Gd, grant grace to my bereft soul.

19 Suffering Prayer

Summary:	A prayer for those who suffer intense physical pain
Used for:	Request for the alleviation of suffering
Length of prayer:	Short
Special requirements:	None
Author:	Rabbi Eryn London
Original language:	English

This prayer seeks to address the experience of deep emotional, spiritual or physical distress. It can be recited from the point of view of the chaplain or the patient.

Please be in the hearts and lives of all those who are suffering.

Bring healing to those who are enduring pain.

Bring value to those who are disregarded.

Bring joy to those in great sorrow.

Bring hope to those who feel they have nothing to live for.

Bring provision to those who are hungry.

Bring shelter to those without a home.

Bring community to those who are lonely.

Please use and prompt me to be Your hands of love across a hurting world.

20 Pain Prayer

Summary:	Prayer from the point of view of the sufferer
Used for:	Anyone in pain
Length of prayer:	Short
Special requirements:	None
Author:	Rabbi Eryn London
Original language:	English

This prayer is a powerful request to ask Gd to ease one's suffering. It is recited by the patient.

Dear Gd, from the depths I call out to you.

And I ask in the simplest of ways, please ease my pain.

This pain takes over my body, my mind and my spirit.

I feel the ache, the throbbing, the burning, the stinging – praying to you that it will go away.

I do not feel like myself.

My mind wanders and I am unable to concentrate.

I lash out at those who try to help me.

I find no comfort.

I long for the day where I feel able to move freely.

Where I do not need to stop.

Where I do not need to rest.

Where I do not need to stay behind.

Where I do not hurt.

May I find strength in my good days.

May I still be able to do what I enjoy doing and be with the people I love.

May I feel like myself again.

May I continue to have good days.

Please hear my cries. Please ease my pain.

21 Pre-Surgery Prayer

Summary:	Prayer before surgery or procedure
Used for:	Pre-operative patients
Length of prayer:	Short
Special requirements:	None
Author:	Rabbi M. Chava Evans
Original language:	English

This prayer was written specifically for people going into surgery. It can also be used for other kinds of procedures when the patient is feeling anxious or uncertain. The prayer aims to soothe those feelings and cultivate inner strength and confidence. It is recited by the chaplain.

Lord,

We know and we remember that You are the rock upon which we stand, Your word is a fortress for our souls and Your promises are a lamp to guide our feet. You remain constant, in a world of bewildering challenges and confusing suffering.

We call and You are there, omnipresent and Almighty, Our Father kind, gracious and merciful. So we call upon You today to be our rock and our strength. Help us to hope in you. Help us to have faith in your promises, help us to feel your loving Presence.

Protect and keep our brother/sister within your heavenly arms. Watch over the details of the doctors' works and the work of the nurses. Bring them safely through this time into Your streams of recovery, refreshment and restoration.

In Your holy name we pray, and let us say, Amen.

22 Prayer for a Covid Patient on a Ventilator

Summary:	Request for Divine Presence during a lonely illness and possible death
Used for:	Covid patients, serious virus patients, or those with no family/friends around
Length of prayer:	Short
Special requirements:	None
Source:	Rabbi M. Chava Evans
Original language:	English

This prayer was written in 2020 at the height of the COVID-19 pandemic. This prayer addresses the need for a special prayer for the many ventilated and isolated Covid patients. Now that we are no longer inundated with that particular situation of Covid-ventilator isolation at death, we have reworked the prayer so that it addresses any situation that involves serious illness and loneliness. It is recited by the chaplain.

Lord, let [name] feel loved. Gd. Let him/her/them know and feel how much she/he/they is/are loved, despite the absence of those dear to he/her/them. Let [name] feel cared for, peaceful under the wings of your Presence.

Lord, only You know how much a parent loves their children. Only You know how each child pulls at the parent's core as though a cord were still strung between them. Each patient is a child of Yours and You love each and every one with a Great Love. Please send [name] Your great parental love and embrace. Be with [name] and comfort him/her/them at this time.

Now, [name] let us slow our own breathing. Let us slow ourselves down enough to stand in the liquid moment. Like a birdwatcher, we slow down enough to listen and to become part of the hush.

Lord, let [name] feel loved.

23 Blessing for Strength, Comfort, and Peace

Summary:	Blessing at end of life
Used for:	When death is inevitable, such as when there is no treatment or chance of healing
Length of prayer:	Very short
Special requirements:	None

Sometimes when there is no hope for healing, we pray using different language. It is helpful to know what situation you are walking into so you can have something like this prepared. It is also helpful, if possible, to ask the patient what they want and need. Below is a sample prayer you can recite for a patient in these circumstances.

I bless you for strength going forward

For comfort

For release from all pain

and

For peace.

Add whatever is necessary in the moment.

24 Prayer for Organ Donation

Summary:	Blessing for organ donation
Used for:	Before receiving an organ/tissue donation
Length of prayer:	Short
Special requirements:	None
Source:	Rabbi Eryn London
Original language:	English

Rabbi Eryn wrote this prayer for cases of organ donation from the perspective of the organ recipient. It is to thank Gd and the donor, and to pray for a successful transplant.

Dear Gd,

I thank you so very much for receiving this [organ/tissue]. Today is a day that I have been waiting and praying for.

In the case of a living donor

Please bless my donor, [name if known] the child of [parent of donor if known]. May they have a speedy recovery, one of mind, body and spirit. I am forever grateful to this act of lovingkindness that they have done for me. Without them, I would not be able to live my life to the fullest potential.

In the case of a deceased donor

Please watch over and comfort the family of my donor. I know that this time is one of sadness and pain for them, but I am forever grateful to them and my donor for this act of lovingkindness. May my donor's name be for a blessing. May they be welcomed under the wings of the Shechina and be treated like the righteous members of society. Without them, I would not be able to live my life to the fullest potential.

With this new [organ/tissue], may I be blessed with a good life, that I should be able to do many acts of lovingkindness. That I may change the world for the better. That I may experience joy and happiness. That I will be able to accomplish what I was meant to accomplish on this Earth. May it be good. Amen

Notes

Part Four:

Liturgical Building Blocks

This section collects some of our most-used liturgical and scriptural fragments. They are building blocks to help you construct a ritual that suits the needs of almost any situation you may face. These texts are not meant to be used as stand-alone pieces, but rather as segments of tradition or scripture that add solemnity and weight to the moment. These pieces can be used in a variety of extemporaneous or creative combinations to more closely meet needs of a specific setting. Additionally, they can be used as a short mantra or song or phrase of comfort for a person to repeat or hang near their space.

25 Shema Koleinu
Hear Our Voice

Summary:	Immediate supplication for Gd to hear our prayers
Used for:	Anything. Can be added to any other prayer that you want heard.
Length of prayer:	Short
Special requirements:	None
Source:	Amidah prayer
Original language:	Hebrew

This prayer comes out of the traditional Amidah prayer and is also part of the traditional liturgy at other moments in the year. It is one of the few texts that invite spontaneous prayer, and can be used as an entry point for any and all expressions of the heart.

שְׁמַע קוֹלֵנוּ יְהוָה אֱלֹהֵינוּ חוּס וְרַחֵם עָלֵינוּ וְקַבֵּל בְּרַחֲמִים וּבְרָצוֹן
אֶת תְּפִלָּתֵנוּ כִּי אֵל שׁוֹמֵעַ תְּפִלוֹת וְתַחֲנוּנִים אַתָּה. וּמִלְּפָנֶיךָ מַלְכֵּנוּ
רֵיקָם אַל תְּשִׁיבֵנוּ כִּי אַתָּה שׁוֹמֵעַ תְּפִלַּת עַמְּךָ יִשְׂרָאֵל בְּרַחֲמִים. בָּרוּךְ
אַתָּה יְהוָה, שׁוֹמֵעַ תְּפִלָּה.

Shema kolenu Adonai eloheinu chus verachem 'aleinu vekabel barachamim uveratson et tefilatenu ki el shomea tefilot vetachanunim atah. Umilefanecha malechenu reikam al tashivenu ki atah shomea' tefilat 'amech yisra`el berachamim. Baruch `atah Adonai, shomea' tefilah.

Hear Our Voice, Lord our Gd, pity us and have mercy on us and receive mercy and favor our prayer, for you are a Gd who hears prayer and supplication. From Your face, our King, do not turn us away empty-handed.

26 Refa'enu Adonai
Heal us O Lord

Summary:	Healing supplication
Used for:	All types of healing
Length of prayer:	Short
Special requirements:	Hope for healing
Source:	From the weekday Ashkenazi Amidah
Original language:	Hebrew

This prayer is one of the most central prayers for healing in our tradition - a piece of the daily morning Amidah prayer that dates back to Temple times. As with the entire Amidah, this prayer is written in the plural form in order to implore Gd to protect all sick people, not just the supplicant. This version omits the formulaic blessing, so it can be recited at any time.

רְפָאֵנוּ יְהֹוָה וְנֵרָפֵא, הוֹשִׁיעֵנוּ וְנִוָּשֵׁעָה כִּי תְהִלָּתֵנוּ אַתָּה וְהַעֲלֵה רְפוּאָה שְׁלֵמָה לְכָל מַכּוֹתֵינוּ.

Rifae`nu Adonai venerape hoshi'enu venivashe'ah ki tehilatenu atah veha'aleh refu`ah shelemah lechol makoteinu.

Heal us O Lord and we shall be healed, save us and we shall be saved, for you are our glory. Bring complete healing to all our wounds.

27 Refaeni
Heal Me, Lord

Summary:	Healing prayer
Used for:	Situations where a short and very immediate supplication for healing is needed. For example, during a code, or in emergency situations in an ER where there is no time to do anything else.
Length of prayer:	Very short
Special requirements:	The possibility of healing should be present; can be used for anyone in any language
Source:	Jeremiah (17:14), revised from Amidah prayer
Original language:	Hebrew

This is a shorter variation of the text from the previous entry. This is quicker and also without a formulaic blessing. It is also written in the singular form from the perspective of the supplicant, and can be used any time.

רְפָאֵנִי יְהוָה וְאֵרָפֵא הוֹשִׁיעֵנִי וְאִוָּשֵׁעָה כִּי תְהִלָתִי אָתָּה.

Refà eni Adonai vè erafe, hoshi'eni vè ivashe'ah ki tehilati atah.

Heal me, Lord and let me be healed, save me and let me be saved, for you are my glory.

28 El Na
The Shortest Prayer for Healing

Summary:	Healing supplication
Used for:	Immediate and direct supplication
Length of prayer:	Very short
Special requirements:	Healing should be a possibility, can be used for anyone at any time
Source:	Numbers 12:13
Original language:	Hebrew

This verse, considered the shortest prayer in the Jewish tradition, was said by Moses when his sister, Miriam, was afflicted by leprosy. We use this text as an example when people feel that their words are not enough. We remind them that Moses spoke five words that were precise and sufficient to express exactly what he was thinking, feeling, and wanting. Let this prayer inspire you and/or your patients to find the deepest and clearest prayer in your heart.

וַיִּצְעַק מֹשֶׁה אֶל יְהֹוָה לֵאמֹר, אֵל נָא רְפָא נָא לָהּ.

Vayits'ak Mosheh el Adonai le`mor el na` refa` na` lah.

And Moses cried out to the Lord saying, "Please Gd, heal her."

29 Ki El Melech Rofeh
You are the Gd of Healing

Summary:	A halakhically-defined blessing for healing
Used for:	All kinds of healing
Length of prayer:	Short
Special requirements:	That the person is Jewish, and that they have not already recited the Amidah
Source:	Amidah prayer
Original language:	Hebrew

This text is the blessing portion of the section in the daily Amidah dealing with healing, parts of which we brought in earlier entries. This version has the words that mark a formulaic blessing, and should be recited as such.

כִּי אֵל מֶלֶךְ רוֹפֵא נֶאֱמָן וְרַחֲמָן אַתָּה. בָּרוּךְ אַתָּה יְהֹוָה רוֹפֵא חֹלֵי עַמּוֹ יִשְׂרָאֵל.

Ki El melech rofe ne`eman verachaman atah. Baruch atah Adonai rofe cholei 'amo Yisra`el.

For you are Gd and King, the faithful and merciful healer. Blessed are You, Lord, who heals the sick of his people Israel.

30

Yehi Ratzon
May Healing be Your Will

Summary:	Direct request for healing
Used for:	Immediate supplication when healing is a viable option
Length of prayer:	Short
Special requirements:	Person's name; can be said anywhere at any time
Source:	Traditional prayerbook
Original language:	Hebrew

This text is a personalized healing text that uses the person's name and implores Gd for intervention using the "yehi ratzon" formula. Variations of this text are recited during Shabbat morning Torah services to ask for healing for specific people within communities around the world.

יְהִי רָצוֹן מִלְּפָנֶיךָ יְהֹוָה אֱלֹהַי וֵאלֹהֵי אֲבוֹתַי וְאִמּוֹתַי, שֶׁתִּשְׁלַח מְהֵרָה רְפוּאָה שְׁלֵמָה מִן הַשָּׁמַיִם, רְפוּאַת הַנֶּפֶשׁ וּרְפוּאַת הַגּוּף לְחוֹלֶה /חוֹלָה [פְּלוֹנִי/פְּלוֹנִית] בֶּן/בַּת [פְּלוֹנִית] בְּתוֹךְ שְׁאָר חוֹלֵי יִשְׂרָאֵל.

Yehi ratson milefanecha Adonai elohay ve`lohei avotay ve`imotay, shetishlach meherah refu`ah shelemah min hashamayim, refu`at hanefesh urefu`at haguf lecholeh(m)/cholah(f) [name] ben(m)/bat(f) [mother's name] betoch she`ar cholei yisra`el.

May it be your will, Lord, my Gd and the Gd of my forefathers and foremothers, that you quickly send a complete recovery from Heavens – a recovery of the soul and a recovery of the body – to the sick person, [name] the son/daughter of [mother's name] [if the person is Jewish] among the sick of Israel.

31 Hanoten Laya'ef Ko'ach
Prayer for the weary

Summary:	A traditional blessing asking for strength
Used for:	People who are worn out and need strength, or who want to express gratitude for strength
Length of prayer:	Very short
Special requirements:	Should not be recited in full by someone who has said the blessing with morning prayers; In such a case, the person can simply omit Gd's name.
Source:	Traditional morning liturgy
Original language:	Hebrew

This text is traditionally recited as part of the pre-Shacharit early morning blessings of gratitude. It is a simple, powerful expression of the need for strength during trying times. It can be recited by anyone, but not twice in one day using Gd's name. The section in parenthesis with Gd's name can be omitted.

בָּרוּךְ אַתָּה (יְהֹוָה אֱלֹהֵינוּ מֶלֶךְ הָעוֹלָם) הַנּוֹתֵן לַיָּעֵף כֹּחַ.

Baruch atah (Adonai Eloheinu melech ha'olam) hanoten laya'ef ko'ach.

Blessed art thou (Lord Master of the universe) who gives strength to the weary.

32 Shehecheyanu
Blessed are You who Kept us Alive

Summary:	Gratitude for the blessings of the present moment.
Used for:	Very broad use, to offer thanks for something new, or for big and small miracles, such as if a patient receives positive test results, or has successful surgery, or an organ is available for a person who has been waiting for one.
Length of prayer:	Short
Special requirements:	If the person isn't Jewish, and it is not being said as a halakhically mandated blessing, then you may want to skip the first words in parentheses and replace them with "Thank you Lord"
Source:	Mishna, traditional prayerbook
Original language:	Hebrew

This text is a popular, versatile, joyful expression of thanks for miracles, good tidings, and new things. It can be used at the user's discretion. Those who do not want to use Gd's name, or non-Jews, can recite it without the section in parenthesis.

(בָּרוּךְ אַתָּה יְהוָֹה אֱלֹהֵינוּ מֶלֶךְ הָעוֹלָם,) שֶׁהֶחֱיָנוּ וְקִיְּמָנוּ וְהִגִּיעָנוּ לַזְּמַן הַזֶּה.

(Baruch atah Adonai Eloheinu melech ha'olam,) shehecheyanu vekiyemanu vehigi'anu lazeman hazeh.

(Blessed are You, Adonai our Gd, Sovereign of all,) who has kept us alive and sustained us, and brought us to this season.

33 Modeh Ani
I Give Thanks

Summary:	First prayer upon rising in the morning
Used for:	Often said with children; may be said when someone opens their eyes from a surgery or a procedure where they have been under anesthetic.
Length of prayer:	Short
Special requirements:	None
Source:	Traditional liturgy
Original language:	Hebrew

Traditionally, these are the first words said by Jews upon arising in the morning. It is meant to reflect the moment the soul steals back into the body after sleep, but could be used after waking up from surgery.

מוֹדֶה/ מוֹדָה אֲנִי לְפָנֶיךָ מֶלֶךְ חַי וְקַיָּם שֶׁהֶחֱזַרְתָּ בִּי נִשְׁמָתִי בְּחֶמְלָה,
רַבָּה אֱמוּנָתֶךָ.

Modeh(m)/Modah(f) ani lefanecha melech chai vekayam shehezachereta bi nishmati bechemlah, rabah emunatecha.

I give thanks to You living and everlasting King for You have restored my soul with mercy. Great is Your faithfulness.

34 Elohai Neshama
Gd, The Soul You Have Given Me is Pure

Summary:	A centering chant
Used for:	Any time it is appropriate to focus on and thank Gd for the gift of a soul
Length of prayer:	Very short; repetitive
Special requirements:	May not be appropriate for use by Catholics and others who do not conceive of the human soul as inherently pure.
Source:	Traditional morning liturgy
Original language:	Hebrew

This traditional morning prayer is a powerful affirmation of life. We call this the "Mr. Rogers' Blessing." Fred Rogers, bless him, used to say to children, "I love you just the way you are." This blessing is a version of that deep and abiding reassurance that one is exactly as Gd made them. The first verse of the prayer can be used on its own as a wonderful repetitive meditation chant: "Lord, the soul you have granted me is pure."

אֱלֹהַי, נְשָׁמָה שֶׁנָּתַתָּ בִּי טְהוֹרָה הִיא. אַתָּה בְרָאתָהּ אַתָּה יְצַרְתָּהּ אַתָּה נְפַחְתָּהּ בִּי וְאַתָּה מְשַׁמְּרָהּ בְּקִרְבִּי וְאַתָּה עָתִיד לִטְּלָהּ מִמֶּנִּי וּלְהַחֲזִירָהּ בִּי לֶעָתִיד לָבֹא. כָּל זְמַן שֶׁהַנְּשָׁמָה בְקִרְבִּי מוֹדֶה/מוֹדָה אֲנִי לְפָנֶיךָ יְהֹוָה אֱלֹהַי וֵאלֹהֵי אֲבוֹתַי רִבּוֹן כָּל הַמַּעֲשִׂים אֲדוֹן כָּל הַנְּשָׁמוֹת. בָּרוּךְ אַתָּה יְהֹוָה הַמַּחֲזִיר נְשָׁמוֹת לִפְגָרִים מֵתִים.

Elohai, neshamah shenatata bi tehorah hi. Atah bera`tah atah yetsartah atah nefachtah bi ve`atah meshamerah bekirbi ve`atah 'atid litelah mimeni ulehachazirah bi le'atid lavo. Kol zeman shehaneshamah vekirbi modeh(m)/modah(f) ani lefanecha Adonai elohai ve`lohei avotai ribon kol hama'asim adon kol haneshamot. Baruch atah Adonai hamachazir neshamot lifgarim metim.

The soul that You, my Gd, have given me is pure. You created it, You formed it, You breathed it into me, and You protect it within me, and You will someday take it from my body and return it to me in the world-to-come.As long as my soul is within me, I give thanks to You Adonai, my Gd and the Gd of my ancestors, Master of all Creation, Lord of all souls. Restorer of souls to bodies that have died. Praised are You, Adonai, who restores souls to the dead.

35 The Four Angels
Beshem Hashem

Summary:	Invoking four surrounding guardian angels
Used for:	Lullaby, prayer of reassurance of Divine protection and presence, comfort
Length of prayer:	Short
Special requirements:	Not recommended immediately following a death or loss.
Source:	Medieval Kabbalah
Original language:	Hebrew

This text, which invites four guardian angels to surround and protect, is traditionally sung as part of a lullaby. For many people it can be used as a reminder that even in dark moments of the night, G-d and G-d's angels surround us protectively. Many Jewish texts bring forth the idea that when a person is ill, the Shechina, the Divine Presence, is sitting in the room above that person watching over them.. It has a very comforting effect. It is traditionally recited in the first person by the supplicant.

בְּשֵׁם יְהֹוָה אֱלֹהֵי יִשְׂרָאֵל, מִימִינִי מִיכָאֵל, וּמִשְּׂמֹאלִי גַּבְרִיאֵל, וּמִלְּפָנַי אוּרִיאֵל, וּמֵאֲחוֹרַי רְפָאֵל, וְעַל רֹאשִׁי שְׁכִינַת אֵל.

Beshem Adonai elohei yisra`el, mimini Micha`el, umisemo`li Gavri`el, umilefanay Uri`el, ume`achoray Refa`el, ve'al ro`shi shechinat El.

In the name of Adonai, the G-d of Israel, to my right is Michael, to my left is Gavriel, in front of me is Uriel, and behind me is Refael, and above my head is the Shechina (Divine presence of G-d).

36 Hamal'ach HaGoel
The Redeeming Angel

Summary:	Request for protection, usually of children and infants
Used for:	To herald a protective force
Length of prayer:	Short
Special requirements:	Usually sung
Source:	Genesis 48:16
Original language:	Hebrew

Many Jewish people recognize these words as a song traditionally sung after the bedtime Shema. For many people, this is a song of comfort reminding them of a time when they were being sung to by a carer. This can also be a verse of hope or connection to Gd. Who is watching over us in our times of need. There are many beautiful tunes to this song that are found on Youtube and elsewhere.

הַמַּלְאָךְ הַגֹּאֵל אֹתִי מִכָּל רָע יְבָרֵךְ אֶת הַנְּעָרִים וְיִקָּרֵא בָהֶם שְׁמִי
וְשֵׁם אֲבוֹתַי אַבְרָהָם וְיִצְחָק וְיִדְגּוּ לָרֹב בְּקֶרֶב הָאָרֶץ.

Hamal`ach hago`el oti mikol ra' yevarech et hane'arim veyikare vahem shemi veshem avotay Avraham veYitschak veyidgu larov bekerev ha`arets.

The angel who redeemed me from all bad, may he bless the children and may they be called in my name and in the name of our forefathers Abraham and Isaac, and may they multiply throughout the land.

37 Nodi Safarta
You Keep Count of my Wanderings

Summary:	Gd is present even in times of pain
Used for:	Comfort
Length of prayer:	Short
Special requirements:	None
Source:	Psalm 56:8
Original language:	Hebrew

This verse can be seen as a source of comfort, as it tells the supplicant that Gd is present even in times of pain. Gd is not only present and watching our tears, but is also collecting our tears and keeping track of our pain and suffering – hopefully to herald an end to our pain.

נֹדִי סָפַרְתָּה אָתָּה שִׂימָה דִמְעָתִי בְנֹאדֶךָ הֲלֹא בְּסִפְרָתֶךָ.

Nodi safartah atah simah dim'ati beno`decha halo besifratecha.

You keep count of my wanderings, put my tears into Your flask, into Your record.

38 Yom Ira
When I am Afraid

Summary:	Complete awe and trust in Gd
Used for:	Emergency situations, coding
Length of prayer:	Very short
Special requirements:	Meditative chanting and repetition
Source:	Psalm 56:4
Original language:	Hebrew

This is a short text of absolute surrender to Gd. We use this as a repetitive chant during codes.

יוֹם אִירָא אֲנִי אֵלֶיךָ אֶבְטָח.

Yom ira ani elecha evtach.

Lord, when I am afraid, I put my trust in You.

39 Adonai Natan
Gd Gives and Gd Takes

Summary:	The preeminence of Gd's will
Used for:	Moment of death for people of a certain faith, such as a Pentecostal Christian or someone for whom Gd's will is central for them or who do not see death as an ending or a tragedy.
Length of prayer:	Short
Special requirements:	Religious beliefs that match the text and an ongoing congenial relationship with the divine at that moment. Should not be used with people who do not share that view. It can be too much or too early for a lot of people.
Source:	Job 1:21
Original language:	Hebrew

This text reflects a particular view of death that surrenders completely to the idea of the Divine will. It may be said at the moment of death for a theistic Jew or Non-Jew, but should not be used with people for whom this idea is not acceptable and perhaps even painful.

וַיֹּאמֶר עָרֹם יָצָתִי מִבֶּטֶן אִמִּי וְעָרֹם אָשׁוּב שָׁמָּה. יְהֹוָה נָתַן וַיהֹוָה לָקָח יְהִי שֵׁם יְהֹוָה מְבֹרָךְ׃

Vayo`mer 'arom yatsati mibeten imi ve'arom ashuv shamah. Adonai natan va-Adonai lakach yehi shem Adonai mevorach.

And he said, Naked came I from my Mother's womb and naked shall I return there. Gd gives and Gd takes. Blessed be the Name of the Lord.

40 Birchat Hatov Vehametiv
The Giver of the Good

Summary:	Gratitude for blessings or miracles
Used for:	Upon receiving good news
Length of prayer:	Short
Special requirements:	None
Source:	Mishnaic
Original language:	Hebrew

This short blessing is used to offer thanks at moments of receiving good news, such as a good prognosis. It is often paired up with the blessing "Shehecheyanu".

בָּרוּךְ אַתָּה יהוָה אֱלֹהֵינוּ מֶלֶךְ הָעוֹלָם הַטוֹב וְהַמֵּיטִיב.

Baruch atah Adonai eloheinu melech ha'olam hatov vehameitiv.

Blessed are You, Lord, King of the universe, the Good and the Creator of good for others.

41 Baruch Dayan Ha'emet
Blessed is the Judge

Summary:	The preeminence of Gd's judgment
Used for:	Moment of death
Length of prayer:	Very short
Special requirements:	Best for observant Jewish people who expect this to be said, as for others it may be awkward.
Source:	Mishnaic
Original language:	Hebrew

Among observant Jews, the tradition is to recite these three words upon hearing of a death. However, from our experience, if these words are said at that moment to people who do not expect to hear them, it might come across as rote or callous instead of empathetic. Use your best judgment with the situation.

בָּרוּךְ דַּיַּן הָאֱמֶת.

Baruch dayan ha`emet.

Blessed be the Judge of truth.

Notes

Part Five

Non-Jewish Prayers Adapted for the Jewish Chaplain

Thus far, we have presented selections of Jewish liturgy that are intended for a chaplain praying primarily with Jewish patients but also be adapted for use with non-Jewish patients. However, to create a shared language that is understandable, comfortable, and meaningful for both the Jewish chaplain and for the non-Jewish patient, it is useful to be familiar with certain texts from Christian traditions as well.

We recognize that this can be complicated for a Jewish chaplain. We also realize that this section does not present prayers appropriate for patients from all faiths. We also recognize that almost all the offerings are theistic in nature. Despite the limited scope of this section and its many challenges, we hope that the prayers we have collected might be of some use.

What follows is a selection of prayers adapted from primarily Christian sources and edited so that they might be usable for a Jewish chaplain. By intention, no overt Christology remains in these prayers. This may well perplex some Christians, but when the only chaplain available at a critical moment is a Jew, everyone adapts. Before praying with Christian patients, we often make a disclaimer, "I'm going to pray in the name of Gd, the Father, I am not going to pray in Jesus' name. Would you still like me to pray?" Most of the time, this is acceptable to our Christian patients, given the circumstances and the options. And so, with the help of these modified prayers, we have been able to serve our Christian patients too.

42 Prayer for the Healing of the Ill

Summary:	General prayer for health and healing
Used for:	Any kind of situation of illness or suffering
Length of prayer:	Medium
Special requirements:	Intended for use by a Jewish chaplain with Christian patients. May be used with non-denominational theists, either Jewish or Christian.
Source:	The Book of Common Prayer
Original language:	English

This prayer is adapted from the Episcopal "Book of Common Prayer" for times when a more formal tone is needed than extemporaneous prayer. The "Book of Common Prayer" is a great resource for rich, complex English-language prayer.

Oh Father of Mercies, Gd of all comfort,

Our help in times of need,

You drive away sickness from our bodies.

You, Gd, will not withhold Your mercy from me. Your mercy and Your truth will always be with me.

And I am poor and needy, my Lord, consider my help and my helper, You, my God, do not delay.

We humbly beseech You to behold, visit and free [name] for whom we are praying.

Your grace and Your truth will always guide me.

Look upon her/him/them with the eyes of mercy.

Comfort him/her/them.

And with Your Goodness Give her/him/them patience from within his/her/their affliction.

Only with the help of Your power

May the sickness be turned to health

And the sorrow turned into joy.

In your time, please restore him/her/them to health,

Granting him/her/them a full recovery of body, mind and spirit

Enabling him/her/them to lead life in service to You.

May all these things be done.

We pray, in the name of Gd, Father of us all.

And let us say, Amen.

43 The Lord's Prayer

Summary:	Traditional and beloved Christian Prayer, touchstone, affirmation of faith
Used for:	Before surgeries and at critical points during one's treatment, often after a prayer crafted for a particular circumstance
Length of prayer:	Short
Special requirements:	Some Jewish authorities do not allow the use of this prayer by Jewish chaplains with Christian patients. Consult your personal religious authority.
Source:	Gospels
Original language:	Greek

Jewish religious authorities differ on whether or not one may read the Lord's prayer as a Jew with a Christian patient. Although we have no qualms about reciting it, if you are uncomfortable with it, you can begin the prayer and then let the person finish it by heart.

Our Father, who art in heaven, hallowed be thy Name, thy kingdom come, thy will be done, on earth as it is in heaven. Give us this day our daily bread. And forgive us our trespasses, as we forgive those who trespass against us. And lead us not into temptation, but deliver us from evil. For thine is the kingdom, and the power, and the glory, for ever and ever. Amen.

44 Prayer for the Dying
Pentecostal

Summary:	Requesting grace at the end of life.
Used for:	Bedside of the dying with or without family members present
Length of prayer:	Medium
Special requirements:	Most appropriate for Pentecostal patients
Source:	Christian traditions
Original language:	English

This prayer, which is most familiar to members of the Pentecostal faith offers many generically religious supplications around themes of life, grace, love, and the Divine, and includes language from Psalms.

Dear heavenly Father, with full hearts we come to You.

You are the almighty creator Gd, holy and full of grace, good, just, loving, and righteous.

We pray that You guard the heart and mind of Your servant [Name].

Lord, they are before You and have confessed that You are Gd of all, and the gatekeeper to eternal life. Father, Your grace and love abound so, take their hands, Lord, and lead them through the valley of the shadow of death, and they will fear no evil because You are with them.

We pray as You take them home to glory to be with You on Your throne that they will come to know Your peace that surpasses all understanding. Amen.

45 Prayer for the Actively Dying Patient
Non-Catholic

Summary:	Prayer of release or commendation
Used for:	Primarily non-Catholic Christian patients at deathbed
Length of prayer:	Medium
Special requirements:	Most suited to a scenario where the imminent death of the ill has been accepted and acknowledged by everyone in the room, including the patient
Source:	Episcopal Book of Common Prayer
Original language:	English

We use this prayer, which has many universal themes around death and mercy, for many non-Jewish patients.

Gd of mercy, look kindly on [name] as death comes near. Release them, and set them free by your grace. Loosen the fetters of sickness, break their yolk of pain, and lead them home from this land of affliction. Be with us as we watch and wait, and keep us in the assurance of your love. Amen.

46 Commendation of the Dying
Catholic

Summary:	A version of the Catholic liturgy before death, to be recited by a non-priest
Used for:	In extreme cases where a Catholic, particularly a Catholic priest is not available
Length of prayer:	Long
Special requirements:	Chaplain must be comfortable reciting these prayers.
Source:	Catholic liturgy
Original language:	Latin

These are prayers that are generally said by a Catholic priest at the end of life, according to Catholic tradition. In consultation with our Catholic colleagues, we understand that this version can be recited in extreme cases by non-Catholic clergy.

Reflections from Rabbi M. Chava

This collection of prayers is an abridged Commendation of the Dying that a Jewish Chaplain can use *in extremis*. Obviously, it would be better if every hospital had access to chaplains of every denomination at all times, but this simply isn't the case. I can't count the number of times that I was on call at a Catholic hospital and summoned in the middle of the night to pray at the bedside of a Catholic patient who was dying. I was told that while only the priests could give Sacrament of the Sick, in an emergency, "anyone" could recite the prayers of Commendation, the prayers said just before or just after death.

When I was first introduced to these prayers, I immediately realized that I could not, as a Jew, recite them as they were full of references to Jesus,

Christology, and trinitarian theology, as well as mentions of the saints and Mother Mary. None of these can reasonably be said by a Jew who believes in One Gd.

But the need for a working knowledge of the prayers to say with a dying Catholic patient was persistent. So I have, with guidance from my Catholic colleagues, composed a version of the Prayers of Commendation free of Trinitarian or Christological theology, without mention of Jesus, Mary, or the Catholic saints.

You have to find your own comfort level in this process. The expectation should not be that all Jewish chaplains are now able to do Prayers of Commendation, as some may not feel comfortable reciting even this altered version. Additionally, some Christian patients may feel that excision of Jesus from the liturgy renders it meaningless. Make it clear from the outset that you will be praying in the name of Gd and not in the name of Jesus. And ultimately you will be your own guide in finding the right path in each situation with each person you serve at this sacred moment.

Short texts

One or more of the following short texts may be recited with the dying person. If necessary, they may be softly repeated two or three times. We usually recite only one of these texts. It may be uncomfortable to use readings from the New Testament, but if you feel comfortable doing so, it is permitted by Catholic Law and by some Jewish legal scholars. We have also included readings from the Hebrew Bible.

Whether we live or die, we are the Lord's. (Romans 14:8)

We have an everlasting home in heaven (Corinthians 5:1)

We shall be with the Lord forever. (Thessalonians 4:17)

We shall see Gd as he really is. (1 John 3:2)

We have passed from death to love because we love each other. (John 3:14)

To you Lord, I lift up my soul. (Psalms 25:1)

The Lord is my light and my salvation (Psalm 27:1)

I believe that I shall see the goodness of the Lord in the land of the living. (Psalm27:13)

My soul thirsts for the living Gd. (Psalms 42:3)

Though I walk through the shadow of death, I will fear no evil, for you are with me. (Psalm 23:4)

Into your hand I commend my spirit (Psalm 31:5)

Selected readings

Job 19

Job said: Oh would that my words were written down! Would that they were inscribed in a record: That with an iron chisel and lead they were cut in the rock forever. But as for me I know that my Redeemer lives, and that he will at last stand forth upon the dust. Whom I myself shall see: my own eyes and not another shall behold him. And from my flesh I shall see Gd; my innermost being is consumed with longing. This is the word of the Lord. (Job 19;23-29)

Psalm 23

The Lord is my shepherd; I shall not want. He makes me lie down in pastures green and he leads me beside the still waters; he refreshes my soul. He guides me in the right paths for his name's sake. Even as I walk through the valley of the shadow of death, I will fear no evil; for you are at my side, with your rod and your staff that give me courage. You spread the table before me, in sight of my foes; you anoint my head with oil; my cup overflows. Only goodness and kindness follow me all the days of my life; And I shall dwell in the house of the Lord for years to come.

Psalm 121

I lift up my eyes towards the mountains; from where will come my help? My help is from the Lord who made heaven and earth. May he not suffer your foot to slip; may he slumber not who guards you. Indeed he neither slumbers nor sleeps, the guardian of Israel.

The Lord is your guardian, the Lord is your shade. He is beside you at your right hand. The Lord will guard you from all evil; he will guard your life. The Lord will guide both your coming and you're going both now and forever.

John 4:16

We have come to believe in the love that Gd has for us. Gd is love, and he who abides in love, abides in Gd and Gd in him.

John 14:27

Peace is my farewell to you. My peace is my gift to you. I do not give it to you as the world gives peace, but you give it whole and complete. Do not be distressed or fearful.

Prayer of Commendation Proper (Catholic)

This is the core text of the Prayers of Commendation. While the preceding short texts and readings can be chosen or omitted as needed, this prayer is compulsory and must be included.

I commend you, my dear brother/sister, to Almighty Gd, and entrust you to your Creator. May you return to Him, who formed you from the dust of the earth.

May Gd forgive all your sins and set you among all he has chosen. May you see your redeemer face to face and enjoy the vision of Gd forever.

Welcome your servant, Lord, into the place of salvation which because of your mercy he/she rightly hoped for.

Amen.

Deliver your Servant

Deliver your servant Lord, from every distress.
Amen.

Deliver your servant Lord, as you delivered Noah from the flood.
Amen.

Deliver your servant Lord, as you delivered Job from his sufferings.
Amen.

Deliver your servant Lord, as you delivered Moses from the hands of Pharaoh.
Amen.

Deliver your servant Lord, as you delivered Daniel from the lion's den.
Amen.

Deliver your servant, Lord, as you delivered David from the attacks of Saul and Goliath.
Amen.

Deliver your servant Lord, in peace and in love, deliver him.
Amen.

47 Catholic Prayer after Death
Abridged

Summary:	Post-mortem Prayer, Catholic
Used for:	Immediately after death
Length of prayer:	Short/medium
Special requirements:	Most appropriate for Catholic patients
Source:	Catholic tradition
Original language:	Latin

When death has occurred, the following prayer, as well as a prayer of commendation, may be recited.

Let us pray.

All powerful, and merciful Gd,

We commend to you [name], your servant,

In your mercy and love,

Blot out the sins he/she has committed

Through human weakness.

In this world he/she has died;

Let him/her live with you forever.

We ask this of our faithful Gd, Amen.

48 Prayer for the Recently Bereft

Summary:	Post-mortem prayer focusing on the mourners
Used for:	Non-Catholic Christians
Length of prayer:	Medium
Special requirements:	Chaplain must be comfortable saying this
Source:	Adapted from the book of Common Prayer
Original language:	English

This prayer is intended to be used in conjunction with prayers for the recently deceased. It is important to remember, directly after a death, to pray both for the soul of the dead and for those left behind. This prayer focuses on the latter.

As for those who remain here,

Help us through our valley of sorrows.

In time, grant us healing from our loss.

Let us remember our (brother/sister/spouse/parent/etc)

and all he/she/they meant to us.

May his/her/their memory be for a blessing forever.

Grant us some peace knowing

Our loved one reside now with you

In peace and in love.

49 Prayer for those who Mourn

Summary:	A variation of the prayer that focuses on the mourner
Used for:	Immediately after the death of a loved one
Length of prayer:	Medium
Special requirements:	None
Source:	Cited in New York Presbyterian Hospital chaplain booklet/literature
Original language:	English

Gracious Gd, we come before you in pain and sorrow.

We grieve the loss [name], a precious human life.

Give your grace to those who grieve,

that they may find comfort in your presence

and be strengthened by your Spirit.

Be with this family as they mourn,

and draw them together in your healing love,

Amen.

50 Prayer for the Soul of the Deceased

Summary:	A prayer for the departed soul
Used for:	Christian and culturally Christian patients who have just died
Length of prayer:	Medium
Special requirements:	Chaplain must be comfortable saying this.
Source:	Adapted from the "Book of Common Prayer"
Original language:	English

Let us pray: Almighty and Eternal Gd,

We entrust our (sister/brother/friend) to your mercy.

You loved him/her beyond measure in this life,

Now he/she/they are freed from all cares.

Let him/her/them pass safely into your loving embrace.

Grant him/her/them Peace Everlasting.

Pardon his/her/their sins and grant him/her/them Eternal Life.

So that he/she/they may dwell forever in Your light.

Welcome him/her/them now into Heaven

Where there shall be no more sorrow,

No more weeping or pain,

But only love, peace, and joy

With your Holy Presence

Forever and ever,

Amen.

51 A Christmas Prayer

Summary:	A Christmas Prayer that does not rely on Christology
Used for:	A Jewish chaplain working in a healthcare environment over Christmas
Length of prayer:	Medium
Special requirements:	Chaplain must be comfortable acknowledging Christmas and its role in the spiritual lives of your patients.
Source:	Rabbi M. Chava Evans
Original language:	English

This prayer was composed by Rabbi M. Chava for her Christian patients during the Christmas shifts (which are often largely staffed by Jews). Christians often want a prayer that reflects the day, and it's tricky to give them one without a good deal of Christology. This prayer, which came from working with a devout Catholic friend, uses some Christmas themes in universal language.

Lord, on this Christmas Day we pause to reflect upon and to rejoice in Your many gifts of Grace.

This is the season of gathered light; Lord, bless us all with your light.

This is the season of hope; we pray that hope finds our hearts and the hearts of all who await relief.

In this season, we remember one special family and we pray for the well-being of our families and loved ones. We pray also: may all who are far from home find companionship and community.

In this season, we remember kind men and women who gave shelter to those in need. We give thanks for our homes and we pray that all who stand in need of shelter find it.

In this season, we thank You, Lord, for making Your Presence felt among us. May we feel You with us every day – from the moment we rise until the moment sleep finds us.

Gracious Father, bestow this season's blessings upon us, upon our loved ones and upon our fellow men near and far. For what we have, and for what we are about to receive, Lord, make us truly grateful.

Amen.

Notes

Part Six

Examples of Lifecycle Services

In this final section, we pull together the "building blocks" to offer you several compilations of ritual services for several key lifecycle events. In this section we cover:

- Baby Naming Ceremony

- Emergency Baptism

- Service after a Fetal Demise

- Service at the Bedside of the Deceased

- Compassionate Extubation Service

These are just a few examples that can offer creative ideas and direction for how to construct your own services.

52 Baby Naming Ceremony

Summary:	Blessings and welcomes for the new baby
Used for:	Newborn in hospital
Length of prayer:	Long prayer/Short service
Special requirements:	Advance preparation of materials for participants is recommended.
Sources:	Traditional liturgy along with original prayers by Rabbi Eryn London and Rabbi M. Chava Evans
Original language:	Some Hebrew and some English

This baby naming ceremony can be used in the hospital, though it can also be used elsewhere. It is important to be prepared to do this in the hospital because some families want to name their baby immediately, and others have babies who must stay in the hospital for extended periods. The ceremony can be flexible, with additions and variations, and sections can be recited by the chaplain, parents, or other. You may consider asking the parent(s) or others present if they would like to add blessings for the child.

If it is known that the child will not survive many hours or days, consider skipping or changing the wording of the line "May my child be blessed with health, strength, happiness, peace, and length of days."

Shehecheyanu

בָּרוּךְ אַתָּה יְהוָֹה אֱלֹהֵינוּ מֶלֶךְ הָעוֹלָם, שֶׁהֶחֱיָנוּ וְקִיְּמָנוּ וְהִגִּיעָנוּ לַזְּמָן הַזֶּה.

Baruch atah Adonai eloheinu melech ha'olam, shehecheyanu vekiyemanu vehigi'anu lazeman hazeh.

Blessed is the Source of Life, the Fountain of Being whose power enlivens us, sustains us, and enables us to reach this moment of joy.

Yehi Ratzon

Male:

יְהִי רָצוֹן מִלְּפָנֶיךָ, שֶׁהַיֶּלֶד הַזֶּה יִתְבָּרֵךְ בִּבְרִיאוּת, כֹּחַ, אֹשֶׁר, שָׁלוֹם, וַאֲרִיכוּת יָמִים. שֶׁיְּגְדַּל בִּשְׁלֵמוּת עִם עַצְמוֹ וְעִם עוֹלָמוֹ. שֶׁיַּעֲבֹד לִקְרַאת גְּאֻלָּה שְׁלֵמָה, שֶׁיִּתְבָּרֵךְ בְּפִלְאֵי הַחַיִּים, וְשֶׁדַּרְכּוֹ תִּהְיֶה דֶּרֶךְ שֶׁל יֹשֶׁר, אֱמֶת, עֲנָוָה, בִּינָה, וְשָׁלוֹם. אָמֵן.

Yehi ratson milefanecha, shehayeled hazeh yitbarech bivri`ut, koach, osher, shalom, va`arichut yamim. Sheyigdal bishlemut 'im 'atsmo ve'im 'olamo. sheya'avod likrat ge`ulah shelemah, sheyitbarech befil`ei hachayim, veshedarko tihyeh derech shel yosher, emet, 'anavah, binah, veshalom. Amen.

Female:

יְהִי רָצוֹן מִלְּפָנֶיךָ, שֶׁהַיַּלְדָּה הַזֹּאת תִּתְבָּרֵךְ בִּבְרִיאוּת, כֹּחַ, אֹשֶׁר, שָׁלוֹם, וַאֲרִיכוּת יָמִים. שֶׁתִּגְדַּל בִּשְׁלֵמוּת עִם עַצְמָהּ וְעִם עוֹלָמָהּ. שֶׁתַּעֲבֹד לִקְרַאת גְּאֻלָּה שְׁלֵמָה, שֶׁתִּתְבָּרֵךְ בְּפִלְאֵי הַחַיִּים, וְשֶׁדַּרְכָּהּ תִּהְיֶה דֶּרֶךְ שֶׁל יֹשֶׁר, אֱמֶת, עֲנָוָה, בִּינָה, וְשָׁלוֹם. אָמֵן.

Yehi ratson milefanecha, shehayaldah hazot titbarech bivri`ut, koach, osher, shalom, va`arichut yamim. Shetigdal bishlemut 'im 'atsmah ve'im 'olamah. Sheta'avod likrat ge`ulah shelemah, shetitbarech befil`ei hachayim, veshedarechah tihyeh derech shel yosher, emet, 'anavah, binah, veshalom. Amen.

May my child be blessed with health, strength, happiness, peace, and length of days.

May he/she/they grow at peace with her/himself and her/his/their world.

May he/she/they labor for the redemption of all creation, and be filled with the wonder of life May her/his/their path be right, leading her/him/them to truth, humility, understanding, and peace. Amen.

Parental blessings

For a boy:

יְשִׂימְךָ אֱלֹהִים כְּאֶפְרַיִם וְכִמְנַשֶּׁה.

Yesimecha elohim ke`efraym vechimnasheh.

May you be like Ephraim and Menashe

For a girl:

יְשִׂימֵךְ אֱלֹהִים כְּשָׂרָה רִבְקָה רָחֵל וְלֵאָה.

Yesimech elohim keSarah Rivkah Rachel veLe`ah.

May you be like Sarah, Rebecca, Rachel, and Leah

Priestly blessings

יְבָרֶכְךָ יְהֹוָה וְיִשְׁמְרֶךָ.

Yevarechcha Adonai veyishmerecha.

May Gd bless you, and guard you.

יָאֵר יְהֹוָה פָּנָיו אֵלֶיךָ, וִיחֻנֶּךָּ.

Ya`er Adonai panav elecha, vichuneka.

May Gd make His face shine unto you, and be gracious to you.

יִשָּׂא יְהֹוָה פָּנָיו אֵלֶיךָ, וְיָשֵׂם לְךָ שָׁלוֹם.

Yisa Adonai panav elecha, veyasem lecha shalom.

May Gd lift up His face unto you, and give you peace.

Hamal'ach Hagoel

הַמַּלְאָךְ הַגֹּאֵל אֹתִי מִכָּל רָע יְבָרֵךְ אֶת הַנְּעָרִים וְיִקָּרֵא בָהֶם שְׁמִי וְשֵׁם
אֲבוֹתַי אַבְרָהָם וְיִצְחָק וְיִדְגּוּ לָרֹב בְּקֶרֶב הָאָרֶץ.

*Hamal`ach hago`el oti mikol ra' yevarech et hane'arim veyikare
vahem shemi veshem avotay Avraham veYitschak veyidgu larov
bekerev ha`arets.*

The angel who redeemed me from all bad, may he bless the
children and may they be called in my name and in the name
of our forefathers Abraham and Isaac, and may they multiply
throughout the land.

53 Baptism of an Infant in an Emergency

Summary:	Baptism texts
Used for:	Baptism for a baby who might not live
Length of prayer/service:	Long prayer or a short service
Special requirements:	Water Chaplain must be comfortable facilitating a Baptism, or be able to supervise another person doing it, such as a family member.
Source:	Rabbi M. Chava Evans
Original language:	English

Reflections from Rabbi M. Chava

One of the most challenging situations I have ever been in was in the middle of the night for a baby in the Neonatal Intensive Care Unit. The mother had just been told that her newborn was not going to live more than a few hours. When I met her, she was holding the baby against her bare skin with tears running down her face. She was adamant that she wanted the child to be baptized before he died.

According to most Protestant denominations, with the exception of the Baptists, it is permissible for anyone to Baptize using the phrase, "I baptize you with this water in the name of the Father, the Son and the Holy Ghost." However, from the point of view of Jewish law, everyone agrees that it would be impossible for a Jewish clergyperson to say this formulation with integrity. What to do?

Since it was an emergency, a case of great need, and a situation with limited options, I decided to have the baby's grandmother, a Christian, perform the baptism. I provided a few passages for other members of the family to read, and I offered a brief prayer at the end of the service. With that, the infant was baptized about an hour before he died.

Evocation

The Chaplain recites:

Through the sacrament of baptism Gd's Spirit initiates us into Christ's Holy Church. So, come to the water – water poured over and immersing us, water flowing freely for all who will receive it, water from the streams of Gd's saving power and justice, water that brings hope to all who thirst for righteousness, water that refreshes life, nurtures growth, and offers new birth.

[Name] I baptize you in the name of the father, the son and the holy spirit, Amen.

Gospel Readings

The following readings may be appropriate for an emergency baptism:

Matthew 28:18-20

And Jesus came and spoke unto them, saying, All power is given unto me in heaven and in earth. Go ye therefore, and teach all nations, baptizing them in the name of the Father, and of the Son, and of the Holy Ghost: Teaching them to observe all things whatsoever I have commanded you: and, lo, I am with you always, even unto the end of the world. Amen.

Mark 1:9-11

At that time Jesus came from Nazareth in Galilee and was baptized by John in the Jordan. Just as Jesus was coming up out of the water, he saw heaven being torn open and the Spirit descending on him like a dove. And a voice came from heaven: "You are my Son, whom I love; with you I am well pleased."

Mark 10:13-16

People were bringing little children to Jesus for him to place his hands on them, but the disciples rebuked them. When Jesus saw this, he was indignant. He said to them, "Let the little children come to me, and do not hinder them, for the kingdom of God belongs to such as these. Truly I tell you, anyone who will not receive the kingdom of God like a little child will never enter it." And he took the children in his arms, placed his hands on them and blessed them.

54 Service after a Fetal Demise

Summary:	Blessing and mourning the deceased infant
Used for:	For a stillborn birth, or a newborn who dies shortly after birth
Length of prayer:	Long prayer, short service
Special requirements:	Run your plan by the parents first. Some parts are only appropriate if the family involved is Jewish.
Source:	Some traditional and some original by Rabbi M. Chava Evans
Original language:	English

After a fetal demise or after a baby passes, this is a very sensitive and emotional time for all who are involved. Some parents want a ceremony or ritual marking the death. We recommend compiling a service with a shortened version of the traditional Vidui and El Malei Rachamim, for Jewish families, and a ceremony for Christian families.

The parent(s) may want to give a name to their child. A suggested naming text is included in this segment. If they do not want a name, you can simply say, "The baby of X and Y."

It might also be appropriate to ask the parent(s) or those present if they would like to give a blessing or wishes to the baby.

Prayer for a Jewish Stillborn Baby

Recite one time:

שְׁמַע יִשְׂרָאֵל יְהוָה אֱלֹהֵינוּ יְהוָה אֶחָד.

Shema' yisra`el Adonai eloheinu Adonai echad.

Hear O Israel, Adonai is our Gd, Adonai is one.

Recite three times:

בָּרוּךְ שֵׁם כְּבוֹד מַלְכוּתוֹ לְעוֹלָם וָעֶד.

Baruch shem kevod malchuto le'olam va'ed.

Blessed is the Name whose great kingdom is for eternity.

Recite seven times:

יְהוָה הוּא הָאֱלֹהִים.

Adonai hu ha`elohim

Adonai is the Gd.

Recite one time:

יְהוָה מֶלֶךְ יְהוָה מָלָךְ יְהוָה יִמְלֹךְ לְעוֹלָם וָעֶד.

Adonai melech Adonai malach Adonai yimloch le'olam va'ed

Gd has reigned, Gd reigns, Gd will reign for eternity.

Gd Gives and Gd Takes

יְהֹוָה נָתַן וַיהֹוָה לָקָח. יְהִי שֵׁם יְהֹוָה מְבֹרָךְ. הַצּוּר תָּמִים פָּעֳלוֹ. כִּי
כָל דְּרָכָיו מִשְׁפָּט אֵל אֱמוּנָה וְאֵין עָוֶל צַדִּיק וְיָשָׁר הוּא. וְהָלַךְ לְפָנֶיךָ
צִדְקֶךָ כְּבוֹד יְהֹוָה יַאַסְפֶךָ. תִּשְׁכַּב בְּשָׁלוֹם וְתִישַׁן בְּשָׁלוֹם עַד יָבֹא מְנַחֵם
מַשְׁמִיעַ שָׁלוֹם.

*Adonai natan va-Adonai lakach. Yehi shem Adonai mevorach.
Hatsur tamim pa'alo. Ki chol derachav mishpat el emunah ve`ein
'avel tsadik veyashar hu. Vehalach lefanecha tsidkecha kevod
Adonai ya`asfecha. Tishkav beshalom vetishan beshalom 'ad yavo
menachem mashmia' shalom.*

Gd gives and Gd takes away, may the Name of Gd be blessed. The
Rock, perfect is your work, for all Your paths are just, righteous
and fair is He. Your righteous deeds will walk before you, and
the greatness of Gd will gather you. Lay in peace and sleep in
peace, until the arrival of the comforter, the announcer of peace.

Naming

יַלְדֵּנוּ/יַלְדָּתֵנוּ בַּחַיִּים יָדַעְנוּ, וְנִזְכָּר בְּשֵׁם [שֵׁם שֶׁל הַהוֹרִים בָּעִבְרִית אוֹ
אַנְגְּלִית] זִכְרוֹנוֹ/ ה לַבְּרָכָה.

Our child alive was known to us and shall be remembered
as [name] child of [parents' names, Hebrew and/or English],
zichron/a laveracha. May his/her/their memory be for a blessing.

*Yaldenu(m)/yaldateni(f) bachayim yada'nu, venizkar beshem
[parents' names] zichrono(m)/zichronah(f) laverachah.*

Special prayer

אֱלֹהִים, תְּקַבֵּל אֶת יַלְדֵּנוּ/יַלְדָּתֵנוּ בַּחִבּוּק הָאֵינְסוֹפִי, שֶׁחַי/ שֶׁחָיָה
בַּחִבּוּק מִשְׁפְּחוֹתֵנוּ. הַמְצֵא מְנוּחָה נְכוֹנָה עַל כַּנְפֵי הַשְּׁכִינָה.

*Elohim, tekabel et yaldenu(m)/yaldateni(f) b'chibbuk ha'einsofi,
shechai(m)/shechaya(f) b'chibbuk mishpechotenu. Hamtze
menuchah nechonah al kanfei hashechinah.*

Gd, accept into the warmth of Your eternal embrace our child,
who lived within our family's embrace. Hold them beneath Your
wing.

Special El Male Rachamim for a baby

Female:

אֵל מָלֵא רַחֲמִים, שׁוֹכֵן בַּמְּרוֹמִים, הַמְצֵא מְנוּחָה נְכוֹנָה, עַל כַּנְפֵי
הַשְּׁכִינָה, בְּמַעֲלוֹת קְדוֹשִׁים וּטְהוֹרִים, כְּזוֹהַר הָרָקִיעַ מַזְהִירִים אֶת
נִשְׁמַת [שֵׁם הַנִּפְטֶרֶת] בַּת [שֵׁם הָאִמָּא וְשֵׁם הָאַבָּא] שֶׁהָלְכָה לְעוֹלָמָהּ.
אָנָּא תְּמַקֵּם אֶת הַבְּרִיאָה הַקְּטַנָּה וְהַטְּהוֹרָה הַזֹּאת, עִם שָׁרָשֶׁיהָ
הַזְּעִירִים וְהָעֲדִינִים, עִם נְשָׁמָה כֹּה נֶחְשֶׁקֶת וַאֲהוּבָה, בְּתוֹךְ מְעַגַּל
הַקְּדוֹשִׁים וְהַטְּהוֹרִים, הַזּוֹהֲרִים כָּמוֹהָ בְּאוֹר הַשָּׁמַיִם וּבְאוֹר הָאֱלֹהִים.

*El male rachamim, shochen bammeromim, hamtze menuchah
nechonah, al kanfei hashechinah, bema'alot kedoshim utehorim,
kezohar harakia' mazhirim et nishmat [name] bat [parents'
names] shehalechah le'olamah. Anna temakem et haberi'ah
haketannah vehatehorah hazot, im shorsheiha haze'irim
veha'adinim, im neshamah koh nechsheket va'ahuvah, betoch
ma'aggal hakedoshim vehatehorim, hazoharim kamoha be'or
hashamayim uve'or ha'elohim.*

Male:

אֵל מָלֵא רַחֲמִים, שׁוֹכֵן בַּמְּרוֹמִים, הַמְצֵא מְנוּחָה נְכוֹנָה, עַל כַּנְפֵי
הַשְּׁכִינָה, בְּמַעֲלוֹת קְדוֹשִׁים וּטְהוֹרִים, כְּזוֹהַר הָרָקִיעַ מַזְהִירִים אֶת
נִשְׁמַת [שֵׁם הַנִּפְטָר] בֶּן [שֵׁם הָאִמָּא וְשֵׁם הָאַבָּא] שֶׁהָלַךְ לְעוֹלָמוֹ.
אָנָּא תְּמַקֵּם אֶת הַיְצוּר הַקָּטָן וְהַטָּהוֹר הַזֶּה, עִם שָׁרָשָׁיו הַזְּעִירִים

וְהָעֲדִינִים, עִם נְשָׁמָה כֹּה נֶחְשֶׁקֶת וַאֲהוּבָה, בְּתוֹךְ מַעְגַּל הַקְּדוֹשִׁים
וְהַטְּהוֹרִים, הַזּוֹהֲרִים כָּמוֹהוּ בְּאוֹר הַשָּׁמַיִם וּבְאוֹר הָאֱלֹהִים.

El male rachamim, shochen bammeromim, hamtze menuchah nechonah al kanfei hashechinah, bema'alot kedoshim utehorim, kezohar harakia' mazhirim et nishmat [name] ben [parents' names] shehalach le'olamo. Anna temakkem et hayitzur hakatan vehatahor hazeh, im shorashav haze'irim veha'adinim, im neshamah koh nechsheket va'ahuvah, betoch ma'agal hakedoshim vehatehorim, hazoharim kamohu be'or hashamayim uve'or ha'elohim.

El Malei Rachamim, Gd filled with compassion, dwelling on high, grant perfect rest under the wings of the Shekhinah to the soul of [name] child of [parents' names, Hebrew and/or English]. Place this smallest of beginnings, tiny and tender roots, who was so desired and loved, among the holy and pure ones who shine brilliantly as the heavens.

Prayer for a Christian Stillborn Baby

Rabbi M. Chava composed this prayer for the stillborn baby of a Christian mother and father. Some denominations will baptize a stillborn or will perform a baptism posthumously (Catholics will not).

Lord, Gd, Father of us all,

We stand before you today with baby [name].

Child of Gd, may your spirit go forth in the name of the living Gd. May you rest in the arms of the Holy One, your Creator. May you dwell forever in his light; and let us say Amen.

In this moment of sorrow, Gd is in our midst and comforts us with his word, "Blessed are the sorrowful for they shall be comforted."

Grant that we may hold this child's memory dear, with gratitude for your gifts.

Grant us comfort and healing in time.

Grant us strength to shoulder this sorrow.

Though our grief may seem insurmountable, we know that through your gifts of love, grace, and peace, you will hold us in our valley of shadows.

Gd gives and Gd takes, blessed be the name of the Lord.

In His name we pray, Amen.

55 A Compassionate Extubation Service

Summary:	Prayer prior to compassionate extubation
Used for:	A Jewish patient but can be adapted.
Length of prayer:	Medium-long
Special requirements:	None
Source:	Adapted by Rabbi M. Chava Evans from liturgical sources
Original language:	English and Hebrew

This service was created in order to meet the needs of patients undergoing Compassionate extubation (CE), also known as palliative extubation, which is performed to alleviate suffering by withdrawing the tube to avoid prolonging death. This is a delicate and complicated task and can raise many feeling for both the chaplain and the family. Also note that a person might not die immediately after a CE, so be prepared to be with the family for longer or make sure to check in with them.

Chaplain introduces the procedure:

We have three tasks today.

The first is to say goodbye.

The second task is bikur cholim, a visit to someone who is ill. This is an extremely important mitzvah, commandment, and the idea is simply to be present to the ill person, and to provide comfort. For that reason, I have chosen three short prayers that [the patient] would have known and which we hope bring his soul comfort.

The third task is aiding [the patient]'s transition from living in this world, to the world beyond. In this world he had one kind of relationship with the Divine to an existence in a realm beyond where he will have a new relationship with the Divine. And while Jewish traditions have a myriad of views on the afterlife, the deeply cherished traditional belief is that, after death, the soul enjoys complete and utter shalom, peace, under the kanfei shechina, under the wings of the holy one, blessed be he. We are here to aid this transition.

And with those tasks, comfort of [name] and aiding transition in mind, we will begin.

Give the family space to say goodbye.

Now we will recite two short prayers and a blessing: elohai neshama, then Shema, then a blessing for peace.

Elohai Neshama

אֱלֹהַי, נְשָׁמָה שֶׁנָּתַתָּ בִּי טְהוֹרָה הִיא. אַתָּה בְרָאתָהּ אַתָּה יְצַרְתָּהּ אַתָּה נְפַחְתָּהּ בִּי וְאַתָּה מְשַׁמְּרָהּ בְּקִרְבִּי וְאַתָּה עָתִיד לִטְּלָהּ מִמֶּנִּי וּלְהַחֲזִירָהּ בִּי לֶעָתִיד לָבֹא. כָּל זְמַן שֶׁהַנְּשָׁמָה בְקִרְבִּי מוֹדֶה/מוֹדָה אֲנִי לְפָנֶיךָ יְהֹוָה אֱלֹהַי וֵאלֹהֵי אֲבוֹתַי רִבּוֹן כָּל הַמַּעֲשִׂים אֲדוֹן כָּל הַנְּשָׁמוֹת. בָּרוּךְ אַתָּה יְהֹוָה הַמַּחֲזִיר נְשָׁמוֹת לִפְגָרִים מֵתִים.

*Eloha*i, *neshamah shenata`tah bi tehorah hi. Atah vera`tah atah yetsartah atah nefachtah bi ve`atah meshamerah bekirbi ve`atah `atid litelah mimeni ulehachazirah bi le`atid lavo. Kol zeman shehaneshamah vekirbi modeh/modah ani lefanecha Adonai elohay ve`lohei avotay ribon kol hama`asim adon kol haneshamot. Baruch atah Adonai hamachazir neshamot lifgarim metim.*

The soul that You, my Gd, have given me is pure.
You created it, You formed it,
You breathed it into me,
You protect it within me,
and You will someday take it from my body
and return it to me in the world-to-come.
As long as my soul is within me,

I give thanks to You Adonai,
my Gd and the Gd of my ancestors,
Master of all Creation, Lord of all souls.
Restorer of souls to bodies that have died.
Praised are You, Adonai, who restores souls to the dead.

Shema

אֵל מֶלֶךְ נֶאֱמָן׃
שְׁמַע יִשְׂרָאֵל יְהֹוָה אֱלֹהֵינוּיְהֹוָה אֶחָד. (דברים ו;ד)

El melech ne`eman.
Shema' yisra`el Adonai elohynu Adonai echad.

Hear, O Israel, Adonai is our Gd, Adonai is One. (Deut 6:4)

Whispered:

בָּרוּךְ שֵׁם כְּבוֹד מַלְכוּתוֹ לְעוֹלָם וָעֶד.

Baruch shem kevod malchuto le'olam va'ed.

Blessed is Gd's glorious majesty forever and ever. (Mishnah Yoma 3:8 inspired by Nehemia 9:5)

וְאָהַבְתָּ אֵת יְהֹוָה אֱלֹהֶיךָ בְּכָל לְבָבְךָ וּבְכָל נַפְשְׁךָ וּבְכָל מְאֹדֶךָ. וְהָיוּ הַדְּבָרִים הָאֵלֶּה אֲשֶׁר אָנֹכִי מְצַוְּךָ הַיּוֹם עַל לְבָבֶךָ. וְשִׁנַּנְתָּם לְבָנֶיךָ וְדִבַּרְתָּ בָּם בְּשִׁבְתְּךָ בְּבֵיתֶךָ וּבְלֶכְתְּךָ בַדֶּרֶךְ וּבְשָׁכְבְּךָ וּבְקוּמֶךָ. וּקְשַׁרְתָּם לְאוֹת עַל יָדֶךָ וְהָיוּ לְטֹטָפֹת בֵּין עֵינֶיךָ. וּכְתַבְתָּם עַל מְזוּזֹת בֵּיתֶךָ וּבִשְׁעָרֶיךָ. (דברים ו, ו-ט)

Ve`ahavta et Adonai elohecha bechol-levavecha uvecholm nafshecha uvechol me`odecha. Vehayu hadevarim ha`eleh asher anochi metsaucha hayom 'al levavecha. Veshinantam levanecha vedibarta bam beshivtecha beveitecha uvelechtecha baderech uveshachebecha uvekumecha. Ukeshartam le`ot 'al yadecha vehayu letotafot bein 'einecha. Uchetavtam 'al mezuzot beitecha uvish'arecha.

You shall love Adonai your Gd with all your heart, with all your soul, and with all your might. Take to heart these instructions with which I charge you this day. Impress them upon your children. Recite them when you stay at home and when you are away, when you lie down and when you get up. Bind them as a sign on your hand and let them serve as a symbol on your forehead; inscribe them on the doorposts of your house and on your gates. (Deuteronomy 6:5-9)

The Priestly Blessing

Recite the name of the patient.

יְבָרֶכְךָ יְהֹוָה וְיִשְׁמְרֶךָ.
יָאֵר יְהֹוָה פָּנָיו אֵלֶיךָ, וִיחֻנֶּךָּ.
יִשָּׂא יְהֹוָה פָּנָיו אֵלֶיךָ, וְיָשֵׂם לְךָ שָׁלוֹם.

Yevarechcha Adonai veyishmerecha.
Ya`er Adonai panav elecha vichuneka
Yisa Adonai panav elecha veyasem lecha shalom.

Recite the name of the patient.

May the Lord bless and protect you.
May the Lord deal kindly and graciously with you.
May the Lord grant you his presence and his peace.

And with these words we bless [patient] for the next phase of their journey.

56 Deceased Bedside Prayer
Christian

Summary:	Bedside service for the deceased
Used for:	Immediately upon death
Length of prayer:	Long prayer/ short service
Special requirements:	Must have the texts of the following prayers readily available.
Source:	Rabbi M. Chava Evans
Original language:	English

When a person dies in the hospital, the family members are usually allowed to be with the deceased patient for a few hours before the deceased is taken to the morgue. This service was designed to support the family at that time. We pulled together several liturgical pieces into one ceremony. We include readings from Psalms that speak of the peace and security experienced by those who have died and are with their Maker and also comfort mourners. We recommend discussing the meanings of these texts with the family before embarking on the ceremony.

Recommended introduction

With your permission, I'm going to perform a very brief bedside service. I'll read from Psalms and John. The readings from Psalms speak of the peace and security experienced by those who have died and are with their Maker. For He who knit our souls so wondrously, as the Psalmist says is the same Gd to whom our souls return. As it says in Job, "The Lord gives and the Lord takes, blessed be the name of the Lord."

But perhaps we do not feel blessed when death comes. So, the Psalms serve another purpose: they comfort mourners who miss (name of the deceased). They remind us that Gd is with us in our sorrow. They remind us too that (name of the deceased) is with Gd in a new and beautiful way. She/he feels no pain, only deep peace, and the embrace of Gd's Love.

Psalm 23

The Lord is my shepherd; I shall not want. He maketh me to lie down in green pastures: he leadeth me beside the still waters. He restoreth my soul: he leadeth me in the paths of righteousness for his name's sake. Yea, though I walk through the valley of the shadow of death, I will fear no evil: for thou art with me; thy rod and thy staff they comfort me. Thou preparest a table before me in the presence of mine enemies: thou anointest my head with oil; my cup runneth over. Surely goodness and mercy shall follow me all the days of my life: and I will dwell in the house of the Lord forever.

Psalm 121

I will lift up mine eyes unto the hills, from whence cometh my help. My help cometh from the Lord, which made heaven and earth. He will not suffer thy foot to be moved: he that keepeth thee will not slumber. Behold, he that keepeth Israel shall neither slumber nor sleep. The Lord is thy keeper: the Lord is thy shade upon thy right hand. The sun shall not smite thee by day, nor the moon by night. The Lord shall preserve thee from all evil: he shall preserve thy soul. The Lord shall preserve thy going out and thy coming in from this time forth, and even forevermore.

New Testament Readings (choose one)

John 14 1-8

Let not your heart be troubled: ye believe in Gd, believe also in me. In my Father's house are many mansions: if it were not so, I would have told you. I go to prepare a place for you. And if I go and prepare a place for you, I will come again, and receive you unto myself; that where I am, there ye may be also. And whither I go ye know, and the way ye know. Thomas saith unto him, Lord, we know not whither thou goest; and how can we know the way? Jesus saith unto him, I am the way, the truth, and the life: no man cometh unto the Father, but by me.

1 Corinthians 13:4-8

Love is patient, love is kind. It does not envy, it does not boast, it is not proud. It does not dishonor others, it is not self-seeking, it is not easily angered, and it keeps no record of wrongs. Love does not delight in evil but rejoices with the truth. It always protects, always trusts, always hopes, and always perseveres. Love never fails. But where there are prophecies, they will cease; where there are tongues, they will be stilled; where there is knowledge, it will pass away.

Prayer for the Soul of the Deceased

Let us pray: Almighty and Eternal Gd, We entrust our sister/brother [name] to your mercy.

You loved him/her greatly in this life, now he/she is freed from all cares;

Let him/her pass safely into your loving embrace. Grant him/her peace Everlasting.

Pardon his/her sins and give him/her eternal life that he/she may dwell forever in Your light.

Welcome him/her now into heaven where there shall be no more sorrow

No more weeping or pain but only love, peace, and joy
With Your Holy Presence forever and ever.
Amen.

A Prayer for Mourners

As for those of us who remain, Lord:
Gather us, the brokenhearted, to You.
Embrace us – we are lonely in our grief.
Comfort us – we need Your Peace.
Guide us – we stumble in our sorrow.
Father, we know You walk with us,
We know You mourn with us,
We beseech You: stay. Be with us.
Your Presence strengthens and soothes
So we may bear our pain. Because, Lord?
Today, we do not live, we merely endure.
One day, You will teach us to live again,
Teach us to live with our grief, teach us
How to honor [name]'s memory, with words and deeds.
But for today, Lord, we simply remember [name].
We remember her and all he/she meant to us,
And we grieve. We have no other task.
Henceforth, [name]'s memory will be a blessing:
Inspiring, guiding and sustaining us
Until we join [him/her] in your Heavenly Kingdom.
But for today, Lord, You grant us just this peace:
The peace of knowing that [name] rests with You,
Holy Father, Gd of Love, Gd of Mercy.

Notes

Notes

Appendix A:

Private Mourner's Kaddish

In our work as chaplains, we generally do not take care of funeral arrangements, which is why funeral work is not included as part of this volume. Nevertheless, for some people, the Mourner's Kaddish is an important part of marking death. However, the Kaddish is traditionally recited with a prayer quorum, or minyan, which is not always available at the time of death. When that happens, we use an ancient Gaonic version of the Kaddish that was written to be used for individuals when there is no quorum. It can be a very important text in certain circumstances.

Here we bring you the Gaonic Kaddish for Individuals, prefaced with the standard Ashkenazi Mourner's Kaddish.

Kaddish in Community (Ashkenazi)

המתאבל/ת:

יִתְגַּדַּל וְיִתְקַדַּשׁ שְׁמֵהּ רַבָּא.

הקהל:

אָמֵן.

המתאבל/ת:

בְּעָלְמָא דִּי בְרָא כִרְעוּתֵהּ וְיַמְלִיךְ מַלְכוּתֵהּ בְּחַיֵּיכוֹן וּבְיוֹמֵיכוֹן וּבְחַיֵּי
דְכָל בֵּית יִשְׂרָאֵל בַּעֲגָלָא וּבִזְמַן קָרִיב וְאִמְרוּ אָמֵן.

הקהל:

אָמֵן. יְהֵא שְׁמֵהּ רַבָּא מְבָרַךְ לְעָלַם וּלְעָלְמֵי עָלְמַיָּא.

המתאבל/ת:

יְהֵא שְׁמֵהּ רַבָּא מְבָרַךְ לְעָלַם וּלְעָלְמֵי עָלְמַיָּא.

המתאבל/ת:

יִתְבָּרַךְ וְיִשְׁתַּבַּח וְיִתְפָּאַר וְיִתְרוֹמַם וְיִתְנַשֵּׂא וְיִתְהַדָּר וְיִתְעַלֶּה וְיִתְהַלָּל
שְׁמֵהּ דְקוּדְשָׁא בְּרִיךְ הוּא.

הקהל:

בְּרִיךְ הוּא.

המתאבל/ת:

לְעֵלָּא מִן כָּל (בעשי"ת לְעֵלָּא לְעֵלָּא מִכָּל) בִּרְכָתָא וְשִׁירָתָא תֻּשְׁבְּחָתָא
וְנֶחָמָתָא דַּאֲמִירָן בְּעָלְמָא וְאִמְרוּ אָמֵן.

הקהל:

אָמֵן.

המתאבל/ת:

יְהֵא שְׁלָמָא רַבָּא מִן שְׁמַיָּא וְחַיִּים עָלֵינוּ וְעַל כָּל יִשְׂרָאֵל וְאִמְרוּ אָמֵן.

הקהל:

אָמֵן.

המתאבל/ת:

עוֹשֶׂה שָׁלוֹם (בעשי"ת הַשָּׁלוֹם) בִּמְרוֹמָיו הוּא יַעֲשֶׂה שָׁלוֹם עָלֵינוּ וְעַל כָּל יִשְׂרָאֵל וְאִמְרוּ אָמֵן.

הקהל:

אָמֵן.

Mourner recites and crowd responds:

Mourner:
Yitgadal veyitkadash shemeh raba.

Response:
Amen.

Mourner
Be'alema di vera chir'uteh veyamlich malchuteh bechayeichon uveyomeichon uvechayei dechol beit yisra`el ba'agala uvizman kariv ve`imru amen.

Response:
Amen. Yehe shemeh raba mevarach le'alam ule'alemei 'alemaya.

Mourner:
Yehe shemeh raba mevarach le'alam ule'alemei 'alemaya.

Mourner:
Yitbarach veyishtabach veyitpa`ar veyitromam veyitnase veyithadar veyit'aleh veyithalal shemeh dekudesha berich hu.

Response:
Berich hu.

Mourner:
Le'ela min kol birchata veshirata tushbechata venechamata da`amiran be'alema ve`imru amen.

Response:
Amen.

Mourner:
Yehe shelama raba min Shemaya vechayim 'aleinu ve'al kol yisra`el ve`imru amen.

Response:
Amen.

Mourner, taking three steps back:
'Oseh shalom [during the Ten Days of Repentance, hashalom]
bimromav

bowing three times
hu ya'aseh shalom 'aleinu

taking three steps forward
ve'al kol yisra`el ve`imru amen.

Response:
Amen.

Mourner
Exalted and sanctified may His Great Name be.

Response:
Amen.

Mourner
In the world which He created according to His will, and in which He rules His kingdom, May His sovereignty be revealed. In your lifetime and in your days, and in the lifetime of the entire House of Israel, speedily and in the near future. And let us say, Amen.

Response:
Amen. May Gd's name be blessed for eternity.

Mourner:
May Gd's name be blessed for eternity.
May His Holy Name be blessed and praised and exalted and esteemed and uplifted, and be praised and admired and acclaimed.

Response:
Blessed is He.

Mourner:
Beyond (during the Ten Days of Repentance: far beyond) all the blessings and hymns, may His Name be celebrated and comforted, as is said forever, And let us say: Amen.

Response:
Amen.

Mourner:

May there be abundant peace from heaven, with life's goodness for us and for all thy people Israel. And let us say: Amen.

Response:

Amen.

Mourner:

May the One who brings peace to the universe bring peace to us and to all the people Israel. And let us say: Amen.

Individual's Kaddish

This is a Gaonic prayer that allows for the recitation of Kaddish as an individual and not in community. The text is from Seder Rav Amram Gaon (9th century Sura).

עַל הַכֹּל יִתְגַּדַּל וְיִשְׁתַּבַּח וְיִתְפָּאַר וְיִתְרוֹמַם וְיִתְנַשֵּׂא שְׁמוֹ שֶׁל מֶלֶךְ מַלְכֵי הַמְּלָכִים הַקָּדוֹשׁ בָּרוּךְ הוּא. בָּעוֹלָמוֹת שֶׁבָּרָא הָעוֹלָם הַזֶּה וְהָעוֹלָם הַבָּא.

כִּרְצוֹנוֹ וּכִרְצוֹן כָּל עַמּוֹ יִשְׂרָאֵל.

צוּר הָעוֹלָמִים אָדוֹן כָּל הַבְּרִיּוֹת אֱלוֹהַּ כָּל הַנְּפָשׁוֹת הַיּוֹשֵׁב בְּמֶרְחֲבֵי מָרוֹם הַשּׁוֹכֵן בִּשְׁמֵי שְׁמֵי קֶדֶם, קְדֻשָּׁתוֹ עַל כִּסֵּא הַכָּבוֹד וּקְדֻשָּׁתוֹ עַל הַחַיּוֹת.

וּבְכֵן יִתְקַדַּשׁ שְׁמוֹ בָּנוּ לְעֵינֵי כֹּל חַי וְנֹאמַר לְפָנָיו שִׁיר חָדָשׁ כְּכָתוּב שִׁירוּ לַיהוה שִׁיר חָדָשׁ כִּי נִפְלָאוֹת עָשָׂה (תְּהִלִּים צ"ח, א').

יהוה חָפֵץ לְמַעַן צִדְקוֹ יַגְדִּיל תּוֹרָה וְיַאֲדִיר (ישעיה מב, כא).

'Al hakol yitgadal veyishtabach veyitpàar veyitromam veyitnase shemo shel melech malchei hamelachim hakadosh baruch hu.
Ba'olamot shebara ha'olam hazeh veha'olam haba.
Kirtsono uchirtson kol 'amo yisràel.
Tsur ha'olamim adon kol haberiyot eloah kol hanefashot hayoshev vemerchavei marom hashochen bishmei shemei kedem, kedushato 'al kise hakavod ukedushato 'al hachayot.

Uvechen yitkadash shemo banu le'einei kol chay venomar lefanav shir chadash kechatuv shiru l'Adonai shir chadash ki nifla`ot 'asah.
Adonai chafets lema'an tsidko yagdil torah veya`adir.

Over all may the name of the Supreme King of kings, the Holy One, be magnified and sanctified, praised and glorified, exalted and extolled, in the worlds that He created, this world and the World to Come – in accordance with His will and the will of the whole people of Israel.

Rock of worlds, Lord of all creatures, Gd of all souls who dwells in the spacious heights and inhabits the high heavens of old. His holiness is over the throne of glory and over the Hayot.

Therefore, may Gd's name be sanctified among us in the sight before Gd a new song, as it is written: "Sing to the Lord a new song, for He has worked wonders."

"The Lord desires His [servant's] vindication, that he may magnify and glorify His Teaching."

Appendix B:

Blessings for Caregivers

Part of a hospital chaplain's job is to be available for the people working there: doctors, nurses, technicians, receptionists, security guards, etc. A common misconception about hospital chaplaincy is that it only involves encounters with individuals, and that there is no community formation because there is no community. Nothing could be farther from the truth. A good deal of hospital chaplaincy is with hospital associates and supporting the crucial and holy work they do. Below we have collected a few of our most useful liturgical pieces which are appropriate for use with health care workers.

Prayer for Physicians

This prayer, which is attributed to Maimonides (though unverified), is written to be recited by a physician praying on behalf of other physicians, though it can be easily adjusted to use by other health care workers. We often recite a version of this prayer when offering a reflection at a unit meeting or huddle. We also make it available for the medical staff at the hospitals where we work for their own personal use. There are several different versions of this text. We offer here two in English and two in Hebrew (with translations).

Physicians' Prayer Version 1 (English only)

Lord, You are the Great Physician, before whom I bow. Since every good and perfect gift must come from You, I pray: give skill to my hand, clear vision to my mind, kindness and sympathy to my heart. Give me singleness of purpose, strength to lift at least part of the burden of my suffering fellow people, and true realization of the rare privilege that is mine. Take from my heart all guile and worldliness that with the simple faith of a child I may rely on You. Amen.

Physicians' Prayer Version 2 (Hebrew and English)

אֵל עֶלְיוֹן, טֶרֶם שֶׁאֲנִי מַתְחִיל/ה בַּעֲבוֹדָתִי הַקְּדוֹשָׁה לְרַפֵּא אֶת יְצוּרֵי כַּפֶּיךָ, אֲנִי מַפִּיל/ה אֶת תְּחִינָתִי

לִפְנֵי כִּסֵּא כְּבוֹדֶךָ, שֶׁתִּתֵּן לִי אֹמֶץ רוּחַ וּמֶרֶץ רַב לַעֲשׂוֹת אֶת עֲבוֹדָתִי בֶּאֱמוּנָה, וְשֶׁהַשְׁאִיפָה לִצְבֹּר הוֹן אוֹ לְשֵׁם טוֹב לֹא תְּעַוֵּר אֶת עֵינַי מִלִּרְאוֹת נְכוֹחָה.

אֲדוֹן הָעוֹלָמִים, גָּלוּי וְיָדוּעַ לְכֹל בְּנֵי בְּרִיתֶךָ שָׁרָק אַתָּה לְבַד, הוּא מַעֲנִישׁ וּמְחַנֵּן, מַכֶּה וּמְרַפֵּא. בְּרַם בְּחָכְמָתְךָ אֵין סוֹף רַצִיתָ שֶׁאֲנִי, עַבְדְּךָ הָאֶבְיוֹן, בָּשָׂר וָדָם, עָפָר וָאֵפֶר בִּיכֻלְתִּי הַצָּנוּעָה וּבְשִׂכְלִי הַקָּטָן צָבַרְתִּי יֶדַע עַל גּוּף הָאָדָם וְעַל רוּחוֹ, שֶׁאַתָּה בְּרַחֲמֶיךָ הַגְּדוֹלִים גִּילִיתָ בְּעוֹלָמְךָ הַגַּשְׁמִי. וְהִנֵּה, אֲנִי בִּפְקֻדָּתְךָ, בְּמִצְוָתְךָ וּבְעֶזְרָתְךָ מַתְחִיל/ה

לְרַפֵּא יְצוּרֵי כַפֶּיךָ בְּהַבָנָתִי הַמְלֵיאָה שֶׁרַק בִּימִינְךָ הָרָמָה וְהַנִשְׂאֵת הָהַחְלָטוֹת עַל חַיִים וְעַל מָוֶת, עַל הָבְרָאָה וְעַל חוֹלִי, עַל הַצְלָחָתִי בְּרִפּוּי הַחוֹלֶה וְעַל כִּשְׁלוֹנִי בַּעֲבוֹדָתִי.

שׁוֹכֵן בִּמְרוֹמָיו, מֶלֶךְ חַי וְקַיָם, יְהִי רָצוֹן מִלְפָנֶיךָ שֶׁתִּתֶּן לִי, לְעַבְדְּךָ, לְבֶן אֲמָתֶךָ חֵפֶץ, כֹּח וְיָכוֹלֶת שִׁכְלִית לֶהַמְשִׁיךְ לִלְמוֹד רַפוּאָה בַּאֵין הַפְּסָקָה לְאוֹרֶךְ כֹּל חָיַי מִפִּי רוֹפְאִים נְבוֹנִים מִמֶנִי.

תְזַכֵּנִי לְהַבִּיט עַל כֹּל סוֹבֵל, הַבָּא לִשְׁאוֹל לְשָׁאֹל בַּעֲצָתִי, כְּעַל אָדָם, בְּלִי הֶבְדֵּל בֵּין עָשִׁיר וְעָנִי, יְדִיד וְשׂוֹנֵא, אִישׁ טוֹב וָרָע, בַּצַר לוֹ הַרְאֵנִי רַק אֶת הָאָדָם, אַהֲבָתִי לְתוֹרַת הָרְפוּאָה תְּחַזֵּק אֶת רוּחִי, רַק הָאֱמֶת תִּהְיֶה נֵר לְרַגְלַי, כִּי כֹל רִפְיוֹן בַּעֲבוֹדָתִי יָכוֹל לְהָבִיא כִּלָּיוֹן וּמַחֲלָה לִיצִיר כַּפֶּיךָ. אָנָא יְהֹוָה רַחוּם וְחַנוּן, חַזְקֵנִי וְאַמְצֵנִי בְּגוּפִי וּבְנַפְשִׁי, וְרוּחַ שָׁלֵם תִּטַע בְּקִרְבִּי.

בָּרוּךְ אַתָּה, אָדוֹן כֹּל הַמַּעֲשִׂים וּבוֹרֵא כֹּל הַהַבְרָאוֹת.

El elyon, terem she'ani matchil/adonai ba'avodati hakdoshah lerappe et yetzurei kappeicha, ani mappil/adonai et techinati lifnei kise kevodecha, shettitten li ometz ruach umeretz rav la'asot et avodati be'emunah, veshehash'ifah litzvor hon o leshem tov lo te'avvir et einai millir'ot nechochah.

Adon ha'olamim, galui veyadua' lchol benei beritecha sherak atah levad, hu ma'anish vemechanen, makkeh vemerappe. Beram bechochematecha ein sof ratzita she'ani, avdecha ha'aveyon, basar vadam, afar va'efer bicholeti hatzano'ah uvesichli hakatan tzavareti yeda al guf ha'adam v'al rucho, she'atah berachameicha hagadolim gilita be'olamecha hagashemi. Vehineh, ani bepekudatecha, bemitzvatecha uve'ezratecha matchil/adonai lerappe yetzurei kappeicha behavanati hamelei'ah sherak bimincha haramah vehanis'et hahachelatot al chayim ve'al mavet, al havera'ah ve'al choli, al hatzelachati berippui hacholeh ve'al kishloni be'avodati.

171

Shochen bimromav, melech chai vekayam, yehi ratzon milefaneicha shetiten li, le'avdecha, lebben amatecha chefetz, koch veyacholet sichlit lehamshich lilmod rafu'ah ba'ein hafesakah le'orech kol chayai mifi rofe'im nevunim mimeni. Tezakkeni lehabbit al kol sovel, habba lish'ol ba'atzati, ke'al adam, beli hevdel bein ashir ve'ani, yedid vesone, ish tov vera, batzar lo har'eni rak et ha'adam, ahavati letorat harefu'ah techazzek et ruchi, rak ha'emet tihyeh ner leraglai, ki chol rifyon ba'avodati yachol lehavi killayon umachalah liytzir kappeicha. Ana adonai rachum vechanun, chazzekeni ve'ammetzeni begufi uvenafshi, veruach shalem titta bekirbi.

Baruch atah, adon kol hama'ashim uvore kol hahavera'ot.

Dear Lord, before I begin my sacred work healing the creations of Your hand, I beseech you.

Before Your holy throne, please grant me the course and energy to do my work with faith, and that the desire to acquire money or a good reputation will not blind my eyes from seeing correctly.

Lord of the universe, all of your beings know clearly that it is only you who punishes and forgives, who afflicts and heals. However, in your infinite wisdom, you wanted me, your poor servant of flesh and blood, of dust and ashes, in my humble way with my limited brain, to acquire knowledge of the body of humankind, that you with your great compassion revealed to me in this material world. And here, I am, at your command, in your commandments and with your help, I begin to heal your creations, with the full understanding that I can only do this with your great and exalted Right Hand over me and over the decisions about life and death, about illness and healing, and about my success in healing the ill and my failure in my work.

O One who dwells in the heavens, living and eternal King, may it be your wish that you shall grant me, your servant, your beloved child, the strength and mental ability to continue to learn medicine without hesitation for the rest of my life, and to learn from doctors who are wiser than I.

May I merit to be able to see every person who comes to me in suffering to ask for my counsel as a human being, regardless of whether they are rich or poor, a friend or an enemy, a good person or a bad person. In their torment, they are mere mortals.

Maybe my love of medicine strengthen my spirit, and may truth be my shining light, and my I know no weakness in my work that would being to illness. Please, Gd of mercy and compassion, strengthen me in body, mind, and spirit, and make me whole within my soul.

Blessed are you, Lord of al actions, Creator of all beings.

Physicians' Prayer Version 3 (Hebrew and English)

הִנְנִי מֵכִין אֶת עַצְמִי לְהִתְעַסֵּק בְּאוֹמָנוּתִי, עָזְרֵנִי נָא אֱלֹהִים בַּעֲבוֹדָתִי כִּי אַצְלִיחַ. תֵּן בְּלִיבִּי הָאַהֲבָה לָאוֹמָנוּתִי וּלְבְרִיּוּתֶךָ וְאַל תִּתֵּן לְאַהֲבַת הַבֶּצַע וְלְשְׁאִיפַת הַתְּהִילָה וְהַכָּבוֹד לְהִתְעָרֵב בַּעֲבוֹדָתִי כִּי מִידוֹת הָאֵלּוּ מִתְנַגְדּוֹת לְאַהֲבַת הָאֱמֶת וּלְאַהֲבַת הַבְּרִיּוֹת וְלָכֵן אֲבַקֵּשׁ מִמְּךָ שֶׁלֹּא תִּטְעֶנִי בַּעֲבוֹדָתִי הַגְּדוֹלָה לַתּוֹעֶלֶת וְלַצּוֹרֶךְ. אֱמַץ וְחַזֵּק כּוֹחוֹת גּוּפִי וְנַפְשִׁי לִהְיוֹת תָּמִיד מוּכָנ/ה לְהוֹשִׁיעַ לַדַּל וּלְעָשִׁיר, לַטּוֹב וּלְרַע, לָאוֹהֵב וּלְשׂוֹנֵא, וְכִי אֶרְאֶה תָּמִיד בַּחוֹלֶה אוֹ בַּחוֹלָה רַק אֶת הָאָדָם, תֵּן בְּלֵב חוֹלַי הָאֱמוּנָה בִּי. תֵּן בְּלִיבִּי לִשְׁמוֹעַ בְּקוֹל חֲכָמִים אֲמִיתִּיִים בְּנֵי אוֹמָנוּתִי הַחֲפֵצִים לְלָמְדֵנִי בִּינָה כִּי שָׂדֶה הַחַכְמָה גָּדוֹל וְרָחָב. חַזְּקֵנִי נָא וְאַמֵּץ לְבָבִי נֶגֶד הַשּׁוֹטִים הַמִּתְחַכְּמִים הַנּוֹתְנִים בְּדוֹפִי שֶׁלֹּא אָסוּר מִדֶּרֶךְ הָאֱמֶת בְּלִי מַשּׂוֹא פָּנִים. אָמֵן.

Hineni mechin et atzmi lehit'assek be'ummanuti, azereni na elohm ba'avodati ki atzliach. Ten belibi ha'ahavah la'ummanuti uleveriyutecha ve'al titten le'ahavat habbetza velish'ifat hattehilah vehakkavod lehit'arev ba'avodati ki midot ha'ellu mitnaggedot le'ahavat ha'emet ule'ahavat habberiyyot velachen avakkesh mimmecha shello tit'ani ba'avodati haggedolah latto'elet velatzorech. Ematz vechazak kochot gufi venafshi lihyot tamid muchan/adonai lehoshia' laddal ule'ashir, lattov ulera, la'ohev ulesone, vechi er'eh tamid bacholeh v bacholah rak et ha'adam, ten belev choli ha'emunah bi. Ten belibi lishmoa' bekol chachamim amitiyyim benei avmanuti hachafatzim lelamedeni binah ki sadeh hachachamah gadol verachav. Chazekeni na ve'amatz levavi neged hashotim hammetuchkamim hannotenim bedofi shello asur midderech ha'emet beli masho panim. Amen.

As I prepare myself to work in my craft, please help me, O Lord, in my work so that I may succeed.

Place in my heart the love of my craft and love of humanity, and do not let greed, ambition, or glory interfere with my work because these qualities go against the love of truth and the love of humanity. Therefore I beseech you not to misguide me in this great work that I do out of purpose and need.

May I always have physical and emotional strength and courage to be prepared to reach out my hand to rich or poor, good or bad, friend or enemy, and may I always see the ill as fellow humans, and may you place in their hearts trust for me.

Please enable my heart to hear the words of the truly wise in my profession, those who wish to teach me wisdom, because the field of knowledge is great and wide. Strengthen my heart against those who are foolish or dishonest, that I shall not stray from the true path. Amen.

Nurses' Week: Anointing the Hands

It has become increasingly common for hospitals to hold a "blessing of the hands" ceremony during Nurses' Week, in the early spring. At some Catholic hospitals, the Catholic priests will bless oil and then anoint the hands, or some will hold handwashing ceremonies in place of anointings. There is nothing to prohibit Jewish clergy from performing some version of this ritual as long as you do not use the oil blessed by officiants of other religious traditions. If you choose to perform an anointing ritual, it is best to use olive oil whose provenance you know.

We have created and included a version of this blessing of the hands, and it can be lengthened or shortened as needed. Usually, we read the first text to the assembled and then only say the short verses over each individual blessing of hands.

You are Gd's hands in this healing place. May you be upheld and comforted by the assurance of Gd's constant presence at your side and of Gd's healing strength in your hands. I bless your hands and the work of your hands that you might be a healing blessing to others.

יְהִי רָצוֹן מִלְּפָנֶיךָ יְהֹוָה אֱלֹהֵינוּ שֶׁתִּשְׁלַח בְּרָכָה בְּמַעֲשֵׂה יָדֵינוּ.

Yehi ratson milefanecha `Adonai `eloheinu shetishlach berachah bema'aseh yadeinu.

May it be your will, master of the universe, may you bring blessing to the work of my hands.

וַיְהִי נֹעַם אֲדֹנָי אֱלֹהֵינוּ עָלֵינוּ וּמַעֲשֵׂה יָדֵינוּ כּוֹנְנָה עָלֵינוּ וּמַעֲשֵׂה יָדֵינוּ כּוֹנְנֵהוּ.(תהילים צ, י״ז)

Vayehi no'am Adonai `eloheinu aleinu uma'aseh yadeinu konenah aleinu uma'aseh yadeinu konenehu.

May the favor of the Lord, our Gd, be upon us, and let the work of our hands prosper, O prosper the work of our hands. (Psalm 90:17)

יְהִי רָצוֹן מִלְּפָנֶיךָ יְהֹוָה אֱלֹהַי שֶׁיְּהֵא עֵסֶק זֶה לִי לִרְפוּאָה, וּתְרַפְּאֵנִי. כִּי אֵל רוֹפֵא נֶאֱמָן אָתָּה וּרְפוּאָתְךָ אֱמֶת, לְפִי שֶׁאֵין דַּרְכָּן שֶׁל בְּנֵי אָדָם לְרַפֹּאות אֶלָּא שֶׁנָּהֲגוּ.

Yehi ratson milefanecha Adonai elohay sheyehe` 'esek zeh li lirfu`ah, uterape`eni. Ki `el rofe` ne`eman atah urefu`atecha emet, lefi she`ein darkan shel benei adam lerap`ot ela` shenahagu.

May it be Your will, O Lord my Gd, that this enterprise be for healing and that You should heal me. As You are a faithful Gd of healing and Your healing is truth.

Closing Prayer

said in unison

With this blessing we pray that our hands and hearts are strengthened for the work that lies ahead. We pray that we are compassionate in human need , tender and strong in our care for one another. May we be faithful to the commitment to the special ministry of healing.

Night Shift: For Those who Labor at Night

This prayer was written by Rabbi M. Chava in order to respect, acknowledge, and bless the night shift workers.

Gd, remember those who toil at night.
Remember those who work while I eat and rest.
Bless those whose labor is cloaked in darkness
and bless those who go unseen during night hours.
Especially abide with those who care for the ill.
Sharpen their senses and minds to meet the challenges
of their charges
and bless them with rest when their watch has ended.
Blessed are you Lord, who gives strength to the weary.

Appendix C:

Caring for the Deceased Jewish Patient

Below are some general guidelines for caring for a deceased Jewish patient. The guidelines where you are based might be different, especially concerning the discharge of the deceased person.

Caring for the Deceased Jewish Patient

Covering the body

It is customary to cover the body with a clean white sheet.

Guarding the body

Many Jewish people have the custom of not leaving the body alone until burial. They might request to stay in the room or right outside the room until the body is picked up by the funeral home. As a chaplain you might need to help facilitate this, working both with the family and the facility staff.

Shabbat

Some Jewish people will not use the phone on Shabbat or Jewish holidays and will not make the call until after the Sabbath or holiday. Let the staff know. Some will make prior arrangements for "worst-case scenario" so the hospital staff will know what to do.

Synagogue and rabbi

If the family belongs to a synagogue or has their own rabbi, encourage the family to contact their synagogue or rabbi for guidance.

Funeral home

If the family knows the Jewish funeral home they will be working with, encourage them to call the Jewish funeral home as soon as possible. The funeral home will help guide the family with many of the technical details following the death of a patient.

Burial

If the family wants to have a traditional Jewish burial, explain to the nursing staff that they should disconnect the machinery but should not extubate, clean the body, or change the sheets. Funeral homes will work with the chevra kadisha, the Jewish burial society, who will ritually wash and prepare the body for burial. The nursing staff can and should shut the eyes and mouth of the deceased.

Death certificate

Encourage staff to expedite the signing of a death certificate. Many Jewish funeral homes will not go to the hospital until they confirm the death certificate has been signed.

Reciting Psalms

It is customary to recite Psalms at this time.

Finding what you Need

In the following pages you will find several resources to help you find what you need.

The first is an Index of Events. Here you will find suggested texts to meet the needs of particular contexts -- such as birth, pre-op, etc.

The next is an alphabetical list of prayers.

Then there is a list of external references that you may find useful.

Finally there is a standard index.

Hopefully these will help you find what you need easily.

Index of Events

Event	Traditional prayers	Psalms	Original prayers	Building blocks	Non-Jewish texts
Awaiting a diagnosis or prognosis	Shema	Psalm 21: Esa Einay, I will lift my eyes to the hills		Shema Shema Koleinu Heal me, Lord The Shortest Prayer Refa'enu Adonai Ki el Melech Rofeh Yehi Ratzon B'shem Hashem	Prayer for the Healing of the Ill
Birth of a baby			Baby naming	Shehecheyanu Hamal'ach HaGoel	
Child in hospital	Prayer for healing	Psalm 21: Esa Einay, I will lift my eyes to the hills		Hamal'ach HaGoel Shema Koleinu Heal me, Lord The Shortest Prayer Refa'enu Adonai Ki el Melech Rofeh Yehi Ratzon B'shem Hashem Nodi Safarta	Prayer for the Healing of the Ill

Event	Traditional prayers	Psalms	Original prayers	Building blocks	Non-Jewish texts
Coding		Psalms – for some it is traditional to recite Psalms in a time of need		Yom Ira Beshem Hashem	Prayer for the Healing of the Ill The Lord's Prayer
Comforting anxious family		Psalm 23: the Lord is My Shepherd Psalm 21: Esa Einay, I will life my eyes to the hills		Shema Koleinu Ki el Melech Rofeh Blessing for the Weary B'shem Hashem Nodi Safarta	Prayer for the Healing of the Ill The Lord's Prayer (In the Service at the Bedside of a Deceased Christian Woman) Prayer for Mourners
Covid	Prayer for healing the ill		Prayer for a Covid patient on a ventilator	Shema Koleinu Refa'enu Adonai Ki el Melech Rofeh Yehi Ratzon Blessing for the Weary Nodi Safarta	Prayer for the Healing of the Ill

Event	Traditional prayers	Psalms	Original prayers	Building blocks	Non-Jewish texts
Deep despair		Psalm 130: Mima'amakim From the depths I call to you	Balms Pain Prayer Suffering prayer	Shema Koleinu Refa'enu Adonai Ki el Melech Rofeh Blessing for the Weary Nodi Safarta	Prayer for the Healing of the Ill
Digestive tract issues	Asher Yatzar Prayer for healing the ill			Heal me, Lord Shema Koleinu The Shortest Prayer Refa'enu Adonai Yehi Ratzon	Prayer for the Healing of the Ill
Discharge from hospital	Tefillat Haderech			B'shem Hashem	

Event	Traditional prayers	Psalms	Original prayers	Building blocks	Non-Jewish texts
Emotional or spiritual distress		Psalm 23: the Lord is My Shepherd Psalm 63: My soul thirsts for you Psalm 91: Yoshev B'seter	Balms Pain Prayer Suffering prayer	Heal Me, Lord The Shortest Prayer Shema Koleinu Refa'enu Adonai Ki el Melech Rofeh Yehi Ratzon Blessing for the Weary B'shem Hashem Nodi Safarta	Prayer for the Healing of the Ill The Lord's Prayer
End of life/ Deathbed	Shema	Psalm 23: the Lord is My Shepherd Psalm 121: Shir Lama'a lot Psalm 23: The Lord is My Shepherd Paslm 91: Yoshev B'seter		Gd Gives and Gd Takes (for people of a certain faith)	The Lord's Prayer Prayer for the Dying (Pentecostal) Commendation of the Dying (Catholic) Deliver You Servant

Event	Traditional prayers	Psalms	Original prayers	Building blocks	Non-Jewish texts
Extubation	Shalom Aleichem The Priestly Blessing Elohai Neshama		A Compassionate Extubation Ceremony	Shema Koleinu Refa'enu Adonai Ki el Melech Rofeh Yehi Ratzon Mode Ani	Prayer for the Healing of the Ill
General blessing	The Priestly Blessing		Blessing for Strength, Comfort, and Peace	Shehecheyanu Shema Koleinu Blessing for the Weary Elohai Neshama B'shem Hashem Hamal'ach HaGoel	The Lord's Prayer
Illness when there is hope for recovery	Misheberach (for Jews) or Misheberach for non-Jews			Heal me, Lord The Shortest Prayer Shema Koleinu Refa'enu Adonai Ki el Melech Rofeh Yehi Ratzon	Prayer for the Healing of the Ill

Event	Traditional prayers	Psalms	Original prayers	Building blocks	Non-Jewish texts
Illness when there is no hope for recovery	Shalom Aleichem		Blessing for Strength, Comfort, and Peace		
Intense physical pain	Prayer for healing the ill		Suffering prayer Pain Prayer	Heal Me, Lord The Shortest Prayer Shema Koleinu Refa'enu Adonai Ki el Melech Rofeh Yehi Ratzon Blessing for the Weary Nodi Safarta	Prayer for the Healing of the Ill
Organ donations	Asher Yatzar Prayer for healing the ill			Shema Koleinu Refa'enu Adonai Ki el Melech Rofeh Yehi Ratzon	Prayer for the Healing of the Ill

Event	Traditional prayers	Psalms	Original prayers	Building blocks	Non-Jewish texts
Post-mortem service	El Malei Rachamim			Gd gives and Gd takes (for people of a certain faith)	The Lord's Prayer Prayer for the Dying (Pentecostal) Prayer for the Actively Dying Patient (non-Catholic) Commendation of the Dying (Catholic) Deliver You Servant Prayer for those who Mourn Prayer for the Soul of the Deceased
Post-op	Asher Yatzar Prayer for healing the ill			Mode Ani Elohai Neshama Heal me, Lord Shema Koleinu Refa'enu Adonai Ki el Melech Rofeh Blessing for the Weary Yehi Ratzon	Prayer for the Healing of the Ill

Event	Traditional prayers	Psalms	Original prayers	Building blocks	Non-Jewish texts
Pre-surgery	Asher Yatzar	Psalm 40: I put my hope in the Lord Psalm 21: Esa Einay, I will life my eyes to the hills	Pre-surgery prayer	Heal Me, Lord The Shortest Prayer Shema Koleinu Refa'enu Adonai Ki el Melech Rofeh Yehi Ratzon Blessing for the Weary B'shem Hashem	Prayer for the Healing of the Ill
Upon receiving positive news – prognosis, organ transplant, or successful surgery			Blessing for caregivers	Shehecheyanu Mode Ani Hatov Vehameitiv	

Alphabetical List of Prayers

References

"Basic Laws of Aninus." *Chevrah Lomdei Mishnah*, www. chevrahlomdeimishnah.org/product/basic-laws-of-aninus/. Accessed 12 Feb. 2023.

BimBam. "How to Say the Mourners Kaddish - the Jewish Prayer of Mourning." *YouTube*, 13 Nov. 2014, www. youtube.com/watch?v=b5dUVhQxLDM. Accessed 19 Sept. 2022.

Duke Institute on Care at the End of Life. *Jewish Ritual, Reality and Response at the End of Life a Guide to Caring for Jewish Patients and Their Families*. 2007. https://divinity.duke.edu/sites/divinity.duke.edu/files/documents/tmc/Jewish-Ritual.pdf.

Eilberg, Rabbi Amy. "Jewish Principles and Care of the Dying." 2001. https://jewishboard.org/wp-content/uploads/2016/03/oa_2001_04_winter.pdf.

"Final Prayers." *Chevrah Lomdei Mishnah*, www. chevrahlomdeimishnah.org/product/final-prayers/. Accessed 12 Feb. 2023.

My Jewish Learning. "El Maleh Rahamim: Learn How to Say This Jewish Prayer." *Www.youtube.com*, www. youtube.com/watch?v=Kzr0io0o1lA. Accessed 12 Feb. 2023.

Ritualwell Tradition & Innovation.www.ritualwell.org

"Shalom Aleichem - שלום עליכם." *Www.youtube.com*, www. youtube.com/watch?v=913jZFL1bdE. Accessed 12 Feb. 2023.

"The Kaddish Companion." *Chevrah Lomdei Mishnah*, www.chevrahlomdeimishnah.org/product/the-kaddish-companion/. Accessed 12 Feb. 2023

The On-Call Multi-Faith Resource Booklet. New York Presbyterian Hospital. Internally published and used by chaplains at NYP

The Rabbinical Council of America: Lifecycle Madrikh. New York, NY, Mesorah Publications, Limited, 2000

Weiss, Eric. *Mishkan Refuah*. Central Conference of American Rabbis, 2012.

"Welcome." *Neshama: Association of Jewish Chaplains*, najc.org/. Accessed 12 Feb. 2023.

Index

Notes